"The singular issue of our time is a deficit of real men. In this powerful book you will find the prescription for authentic manhood, written by a real man. Moms can take hope as they find help and insight into helping their boy become the man he is intended to be."

—**Tony Rorie**, founder/CEO, Men of Honor/Ladies of Honor

"This excellent book will help you understand why your son is acting the way he acts. Rick Johnson gives you great insight into the inner workings of boys' brains and bodies. I highly recommend this book."

—**Jim Burns**, PhD, president, HomeWord; author, *Teenology* and *Teaching Your Children Healthy Sexuality*

Praise for *That's My Son*

"A must-read for every mom who longs to get inside the heart and mind of her little boy and who yearns for the wisdom to see that boy become a man of character."

—**Susan Alexander Yates**, bestselling author

"You will find wise counsel and encouragement in this helpful book."

—**Family Ministries, Inc.**

"As the mother of a young son, I often worry about raising him to become the man I want him to be. After all, men are still a mystery to me, as they are to most women! Rick Johnson is the founder of Better Dads and wrote this book for mothers just like me after realizing the profound influence mothers have on their son's lives."

—**www.girlfriendbooks.com**

"This book is full of delightful, humorous stories that will have moms saying, 'Been there, done that.' Every mother of a son should study this excellent resource."

—**Michele Howe**, Christian Home & School

"Rick brings fatherly and male insight into the intricacies and inner workings of growing boys. Best of all, Rick shares his wisdom about how to make a boy into a faithful and righteous man. To be honest, little boys have made me nervous in the past. With the guidance of *That's My Son*, parenting a boy doesn't seem so impossible after all."

—**Christian-Mommies.com**

THAT'S MY
TEENAGE
SON

Books by Rick Johnson

That's My Son

Better Dads, Stronger Sons

The Man Whisperer

The Power of a Man

Becoming Your Spouse's Better Half

That's My Teenage Son

THAT'S MY TEENAGE SON

HOW MOMS CAN INFLUENCE THEIR BOYS TO BECOME GOOD MEN

RICK JOHNSON

a division of Baker Publishing Group
Grand Rapids, Michigan

© 2011 by Rick Johnson

Published by Revell
a division of Baker Publishing Group
P.O. Box 6287, Grand Rapids, MI 49516-6287
www.revellbooks.com

Printed in the United States of America

Library of Congress Cataloging-in-Publication Data
Johnson, Rick, 1956–
    That's my teenage son : how moms can influence their boys to become
good men / Rick Johnson.
        p.   cm.
    Includes bibliographical references (p.   ).
    ISBN 978-0-8007-3384-1 (pbk.)
    1. Mothers and sons—Religious aspects—Christianity. 2. Parent and
teenager—Religious aspects—Christianity. 3. Child rearing—Religious
aspects—Christianity. 4. Teenage boys—Religious life. I. Title.
BV4529.18.J65 2010
248.8′431—dc22   2010030352

Published in association with the literary agency of Word-
Serve Literary Group, Ltd., 10152 S. Knoll Circle, Highlands
Ranch, CO 80130.

11 12 13 14 15 16 17   7 6 5 4 3 2 1

To Frank—
"This is my son, whom I love;
with him I am well pleased."

Contents

Acknowledgments   11

Introduction: One Foot in the World of Boys
and One Foot in the World of Manhood   15

1. His Changing Body and Mind: What Happened
   to My Little Boy?   23

2. Communicating with Teen Boys: Speaking His
   Language   42

3. Mom and Son: What Young Men Need from
   Mom   58

4. Dad and Son: What Young Men Need from
   Dad   77

5. Healthy Masculinity: The Marks of Manhood   96

6. Emotions: Developing a Healthy Emotional
   Life   111

7. Dangers: There Be Dragons   124

Contents

8. Developing a Healthy Sexuality   146

9. Spiritual Legacy: Of Gods and Monsters   169

10. Building Character for a Lifetime   186

11. Self-Discipline: Train Him Up in the Way . . .   206

12. Leadership: Teaching Your Son to Be
    a Leader   219

13. Things Your Son Needs to Know to Court My
    Daughter   238

Notes   257

•

ACKNOWLEDGMENTS

S O MANY PEOPLE make writing a book possible. Thanks to my awesome editor, Dr. Vicki Crumpton, and my favorite in-house editor, Barb "How Does She Do That?" Barnes. Not only are they smarter than me, but they willingly make me look good (which is really important by my way of thinking), all without even taking any of the credit. I also appreciate all the great people at Revell and Baker Publishing Group who work so hard to produce and sell my books. There are too many to list, but please know that I do appreciate each and every one of you.

Thanks to all the people who support me behind the scenes and help make our ministry possible. Whether you are a donor, a volunteer, a member of our prayer team, or on my advisory board, please know that Suzanne and I thank God for your presence in our lives every day. Without your generous partnership, we could not touch the lives of so many people around the world. I am honored by your faithfulness.

Build me a son, O Lord, who will be strong enough to know when he is weak, and brave enough to face himself when he is afraid; one who will be proud and unbending in honest defeat, and humble and gentle in victory.

Build me a son whose wishes will not take the place of deeds; a son who will know Thee—and that to know himself is the foundation stone of knowledge. Lead him, I pray, not in the path of ease and comfort, but under the stress and spur of difficulties and challenge. Here let him learn to stand up in the storm; here let him learn compassion for those who fail.

Build me a son whose heart will be clear, whose goal will be high; a son who will master himself before he seeks to master other men; one who will reach into the future, yet never forget the past. And after all these things are his, add, I pray, enough of a sense of humor, so that he may always be serious, yet never take himself too seriously. Give him humility, so that he may always remember the simplicity of true greatness, the open mind of true wisdom, and the meekness of true strength. Then, I . . . will dare to whisper, "I have not lived in vain."

General Douglas MacArthur

Many people have said to me, "What a pity you had such a big family to raise. Think of the novels and the short stories and the poems you never had time to write because of that." And I looked at my children and I said, "These are my poems. These are my short stories."

Olga Masters

Of all the animals, the boy is most unmanageable.

Plato

INTRODUCTION

*One Foot in the World of Boys
and One Foot in the World of Manhood*

*Having children is like having a bowling alley installed
in your brain.*

Martin Mull

I MAGINE YOU'RE SITTING inside a darkened movie theater.
The smell of popcorn fills the air and your shoes stick
to the cola-covered floor. Girls huddle together giggling
in the front rows while boys make noise and show off in
the back. As the lights dim and the movie trailer starts,
you hear a deep bass voice booming out of the darkness,
"Imagine a world where a teenage son comes home from
school and does his homework, always gets good grades,
cleans his room without being nagged, has wholesome
friends, regularly showers and wears clean clothes, and

willingly attends church." All the parents of teenage boys in the audience gasp in wonder. A few moms faint at the very thought of such a boy, and even a dad or two wipes a tear from the corner of his eye.

Sounds like a fantasy movie, doesn't it? Some of you might think you entered *The Twilight Zone*. I suppose there are some kids like that, but that hasn't been my reality nor that of most people I know who live with a teenage son. I know some parents whose sons excelled in academics, sports, and every other imaginable extracurricular activity. Some of them went on to attend Ivy League colleges, prestigious military academies, or some other high-achieving endeavor. From outside appearances they appeared to be the perfect kids. Subsequent results proved that not all of them succeeded as well as would be anticipated. But it was enough to make me question occasionally whether or not I was a good parent.

In reality, most of the teenage sons of people I know have struggles and are less than perfect. They act out or rebel by doing stuff like getting body parts pierced, cutting or dyeing their hair into weird looks, getting tattooed, and wearing ridiculous clothing. Many get into their fair share of trouble; some even drop out of school, take drugs, have sex outside of marriage, or lie, cheat, and steal. Frequently when our kids "perform" at a less-than-perfect level, we feel like failures. The teenage years can be a frustrating time in parents' lives. Especially for moms of sons, this time can be confusing, exasperating, and exhilarating all at the same time.

The other reality is that most of the time we are crazy about this boy who holds so much of our hopes and dreams. We love his good habits, like when he does something remarkably responsible without being told. Or when he says,

"Mom, I love you" for no reason at all. His expressions of affection become more treasured as they become less frequent. When he shows courage and honesty, we swell with pride. Our heart melts at the way he looks when the light hits his face just right and we see the handsome man he will someday become.

As parents, we all want the best for our children. We want them to grow up to be healthy, happy, and productive citizens and people. We want them to marry well, have happy children, and live lives of contentment and rich blessings.

The teenage years are a time of incredible growth and change. But this is also a time of incredible opportunity to shape and develop our sons' character. In a few short years our sons go from being little boys to being men. Biological, emotional, and physiological changes are taking place in your son that seem straight out of a science fiction or horror movie (sort of like when Lon Chaney Jr. turns into the Wolfman). It is amazing the amount of changes that take place in this very short period of time.

I appreciate and enjoy boys—even teenage boys. Boys are fun to raise, to work with, to play with, and to just be around. They attack life with an exhilarating exuberance. Their physicality and the headlong dash in the way they throw themselves at the world is exciting to watch and be a part of. *Healthy* boys are life giving and fun loving.

Our son and daughter, now adults, were born twenty months apart. That means we had teenagers and other creatures going through some form of adolescence roaming around our home for close to a decade (although it sure seemed longer). I remember it as a time of great pandemonium interspersed with brief periods of sanity and calm introspection—probably similar to the enormously noisy chaos and violent upheavals that occurred during the creation of the earth. Despite all that, it may have been the most enjoyable period of raising our children. It certainly proved to be the most challenging!

At various times throughout the teenage years, one child or the other was involved in the following activities (the names and sexes have been omitted to protect the guilty, and though we have only two children, I'll simply refer to "another" child throughout): While my wife and I were away at a Bible study retreat, one child "stole" my wife's brand-new sports car and went for a joy ride—at age fifteen! Luckily, sibling rivalry was stronger than loyalty and the other child "ratted" the perpetrator out with a quick phone call—prompting us to leave for home early. Another loaded up our minivan with their "posse" and was involved in an auto accident in a seriously bad part of town. Still another was chased down by a baseball-bat-wielding lunatic who smashed out the front windshield of our car. Another snuck out in the middle of the night and walked clear across town to a friend's house—said child was gone when we woke up in the morning.

Then there was the constant fighting between siblings, the mad rush every day and night across town transporting each kid to and from multiple sporting, church, and school events. As expected, there were the problems with coaches and teachers. The kids fought with one another and argued with us (my wife is convinced one of them may have even peed down the heating vent of the bathroom when they were mad at us). All these events and other incidents too numerous to mention were huge tidal waves of upheaval in our home. This doesn't even take into account the stress on our marriage and the complicating financial pressures of having two active teenagers in the home.

Some of you having read that paragraph are probably scratching your head asking, "Why is this guy writing a book on parenting?" The truth is, all things considered, my wife and I were pretty good parents. Those are just the types of situations you should expect to encounter while sharing your home with these hormonal beings.

A certain amount of tension normally occurs between teenagers and their siblings, and their parents. As teens strain toward adulthood, they want to try new things and experiences. Our job as parents is to let them grow and stretch without allowing things that will do them harm. Patrick Morley likens this experience to that of a pet owner and his new strong-willed puppy. During a walk, the puppy tugs on his leash because he wants to explore the neighborhood. Generally the owner allows the puppy some freedom. Sometimes though he tries to run into a busy street and so his owner pulls back on the leash. But the puppy's not happy and thankful for this safe guidance. He cannot understand why he can't have his own way.[1] And so it is with teens—they often think parents are being too restrictive when in reality we are just keeping them from harm.

Mom faces the challenge at this stage of "letting go" of her little boy so that he can start becoming a man. At the same time, she has to recognize that in many ways he is still a child and needs loving guidance and boundaries more than ever. If she keeps the leash too tight around her son's neck, he will start rebelling in order to satisfy that urge he has to grow up by experiencing life. Sometimes parents walk a fine line between *preparing* their children to integrate successfully into the world of adulthood while at the same time keeping them safe enough to grow up to *be* an adult. Success in our parenting comes when we understand the challenges we face with preparing our teenage boys for adulthood and then develop a strategy to use the influence God has given us as parents.

What to Expect

This book is a follow-up to my popular bestselling book, *That's My Son: How Moms Can Influence Boys to Become Men of Character*. I wrote that book out of my experiences teaching a seminar titled "Courageous Moms—Raising Boys to Become Good Men." I initially taught that seminar to single mothers with sons, but it unexpectedly struck a chord with women of all kinds, not just single moms. Since then, thousands of women (and men) have attended our seminars on this topic. Teachers, grandmothers, aunts, women with male co-workers and bosses, social workers, criminal justice employees, and any women who live or work with men were attracted to the message of what makes males tick. Many of the women, especially those raised without a father or brothers in their lives, were eager to learn how to communicate with males and how to teach them fundamental traits such as respect, self-discipline, and honor. Most of these women tell me that the information in that book and seminar helped them understand not only their son better but also their husbands, bosses, brothers, and fathers.

Some people commented that my first book was geared toward single mothers, and in fact it did start out that way. This book too will address issues faced by boys who do not have healthy male role models in their lives. The truth is, our country is producing many "fatherless" boys through a variety of family styles and structures. Many married women who would deny that their sons are fatherless are in reality raising their sons as single mothers—children of men who are workaholics, abusive, addicted, or just plain emotionally uninvolved are just as fatherless as children whose fathers are physically absent. Boys raised without positive male mentors are like ships without rudders, doomed to drift along wherever the cultural winds and waves take them. Not only that, but a son has a propensity to mimic the behaviors that were modeled for him by the men in his life—good or bad.

Getting Down to Specifics

My goal with this book is to help moms understand a vision for raising their sons to not just be men or even good men, but to be great men. Our country desperately needs great men. Families need great husbands and fathers. Our communities need great male leaders. Our government, businesses, and churches need great men to be involved. The litmus test I kept in mind was to raise young men who would meet my standards of approval in order to marry my daughter. However, I realize this is a tall order that would make for a very short list of candidates. Nevertheless, if we do not have high expectations for the kind of men we produce as a society, we will reap what we sow.

That first book lays the foundation of boyhood and masculinity that this book magnifies and builds upon. I didn't want to repeat everything I wrote in *That's My Son* (I hate it when authors do that), so it would be a good idea to read—or reread—my previous book before starting this one.

This new book will help you understand the specific physical, mental, psychological, and emotional changes your son is going through as a teenager. It will help you understand how best to communicate with him and what character traits he needs to develop in order to become a healthy man who blesses those around him. In addition, it will point out destructive or even dangerous characteristics that your son needs to be aware of on the road to manhood. It will help you recognize the differences between your feminine world and the world of men that your son is about to join. You will better understand the challenges your son faces with his developing sexuality—a factor that will influence every aspect of his entire being for the rest of his life.

From my research and experiences, it seems that there are three main factors (or pillars of success) that contribute most importantly to a boy being raised into a healthy man: education, character, and life skills. Keep those factors in the back of your mind while reading through this book. Most of the material in this book will be encouraging and inspiring to you, but some of the topics may make you a bit uncomfortable. But don't let that discourage you. Remember, just because we don't like something doesn't mean it isn't true. Better to be uncomfortable than to have painful regrets later. People who ignore inconvenient truths do so at their own peril. But at the very least you will have an accurate, if sometimes frightening, look inside your teenage son. You can then take those insights and use your natural gifts as a woman and a mother to help him develop into the kind of man who will make the world a better place just by his presence—a man who a mother can be proud to call her son.

1

HIS CHANGING BODY AND MIND

What Happened to My Little Boy?

If you have never been hated by your child, you have never been a parent.

Bette Davis

DURING CHRISTMAS THIS year, my sister rented a luxury bus to take all twenty-three members of the extended family to the magnificently opulent and historic Pantages Theatre in downtown Hollywood to watch a production of *How the Grinch Stole Christmas*. As is our inclination, my wife and I sat near the back of the bus in close proximity to all my teenage nephews and their friends (kids generally being more exciting than adults). Interestingly, my young nieces and the other girls preferred to sit up front with the adults, all the while watching the boys with an interested but disapproving demeanor.

Watching the teenage boys while traveling to the theater was hugely entertaining. First the boys explored their ability to imitate animal noises. Their cracking vocal cords made this a unique experience. This quickly devolved into making just plain strange, loud noises designed to irritate any mothers within hearing distance (about two city blocks). Then they spent a significant amount of time trying to gross each other out with words, visual images, and stories about bodily fluids and functions, with vomit and diarrhea being particular favorites. Of course they kept up a running commentary with each boy pointing out the weaknesses and failures of one another. Each boy also performed his "specialty" talent consisting of odd, bizarre, and slightly nauseating acts involving body parts such as leg hair, armpits, eyeballs, nostrils, and tongues. These physical anomalies and parlor tricks were guaranteed to garner the respect and admiration of any male who witnessed them (even I was impressed). The boys told stories of great derring-do where they had risked life and limb to perform a feat with no particular purpose other than to prove their manhood (or stupidity). As things got warmed up, the boys launched into a loud belching competition followed closely by the obligatory odorous contest. Finally, wrestling matches, punching, and general mayhem and torture followed in short order. Thankfully, all the moms were apparently used to this ritualized performance and ignored it, much to our delight. Several younger boys were also part of the group and were excitedly watching and trying to participate in hopes of being mentored in the art of young male tribalism.

As we arrived at our destination, the boys all looked as though they had been run through a hay baling machine, and the moms spent several minutes readjusting their sons' clothing and smoothing down disheveled hair.

Males—you gotta love 'em. As one mom dryly commented while watching the goings-on, "There's not a whole lot of difference between a thirteen-year-old boy and my husband." She's probably right (as evidenced by the movie *The Hangover*). While some of the shenanigans were unique and all were interesting, none was that surprising. Frankly, while a little more enthusiastic in effort, the boys' behavior was not all that much different from that of the men I go hunting with each year. What older men lack in endurance, though, they make up for with years of practice. It's just one of the ways God created males.

The World of Boys

Adolescence is frequently a tough time of life for both boys and their parents. Modern males enter adolescence earlier and stay in it longer than their previous counterparts. (Michael Gurian and other developmental psychologists believe adolescence now lasts from nine to twenty-one years of age.)[1] It is a time when a male has one foot in boyhood and one foot in manhood—a time of rapid physical changes to his body, changes to his brain and the way he thinks and processes information; even his emotions undergo a transformation. It's a confusing time of still feeling like a child sometimes while feeling like an adult at others. Combine that with a male's lesser level of verbal skills proficiency and lack of emotional acuity and he cannot even understand or articulate how he feels about

25

all this. It's scary, thrilling, perplexing, and daunting all at the same time.

The world of boys is probably a microcosm of a man's world, the difference being that because of their inexperience, some of those issues that all males face and struggle with are amplified. A boy's world is one of being afraid of not "measuring up." In a boy's eyes, to be a man is to never fail, to be tough and never cry (at least not in front of anyone), to never give anyone a chance to use or abuse you, to never show weakness or someone will use it against you, and to never ever express your feelings, because feelings are what girls and sissies have.

The world of boys is ripe with sexual tension, homophobia, and fear of peer pressure. To be labeled by your peers as weak, sensitive, effeminate, or inadequate is to invite humiliation and bullying by other boys eager to prove their manhood so they themselves don't become victims. Even the hint of somehow being "less than" a man or overly sensitive or soft is considered a weakness to be preyed upon. Boys with smaller physiques or those who enter into puberty later in life struggle mightily with these challenges and affronts to their manhood. Sometimes the wounds last a lifetime regardless of how masculine or successful a man eventually becomes.

Puberty (Biological Changes)

Between the ages of about nine to thirteen, most boys enter into puberty. Puberty marks the beginning of adolescence. During this time, massive changes take place in a boy's body, virtually transforming him into a man. His body grows and becomes more muscular, his voice deepens, and he sprouts hair all over his body. But while he may appear to be a man physically on the outside, inside he is often still a little boy and now more than ever needs the guidance and direction of a mother and a father. However, even though he still needs his parents, he yearns to start becoming independent in preparation for leaving home. These conflicting cravings can cause confusion and tension between a son and his mother.

Some of the differences we observe between male and female behavior are expressed in common traits. Boys play more aggressively, climbing everything in sight, all the while hitting, running, and jumping at every opportunity. Girls are more likely to play corporately, with the goal being relationships. Females live longer than males and typically perform better under certain stressful environments. Females also suffer more from depression than males. Boys are more prone to be hyperactive and are more nonverbal, later readers, more aggressive, bigger risk-takers, and more adventurous. Males more often operate in a detached and isolated fashion. Solitary work to master a skill is a common characteristic of male life, and men are quicker to dismiss the claims of other people and even of their own emotions. This approach tends to make things (machines, ideas) at least as important as people in the male's inner life.[2]

We used to joke that aliens invaded our daughter's body from the ages of thirteen to seventeen while she was going through adolescence. Miraculously the aliens left just about the time she reached eighteen, and the daughter we knew and loved returned again. While girls are often more dramatic about it, boys too go through extreme changes physically, emotionally, and mentally during puberty.

Adolescence typically consists of early, middle, and late stages. During the early stages (ages eleven to thir-

Physical Changes during Puberty for Boys

- Height and weight increase.
- Body hair grows in the pubic area, under the arms, and on the face, and becomes thicker on the legs.
- Muscles become stronger.
- Vocal cords get thicker and longer—boys' voices deepen.
- The body develops an increased number of red blood cells.
- Sweat and oil glands become more active, and body odor changes.
- Acne can develop.
- Some boys develop small and temporary breast tissue.
- Reproductive system begins to work.[3]

teen) boys are moody, struggle with a sense of identity, and are more likely to express their feelings through actions rather than words. They are less affectionate, their friends become more important, their peer groups are influential, and they recognize that their parents are not perfect. During the middle stages (ages fourteen to seventeen), they alternate between having unrealistic expectations of themselves and having a poor self-image. They also become extremely concerned (obsessed) with their appearance. They complain about their parents' interference in their independence and have a lower opinion of their parents. They strongly identify with their peer group during this stage. During the late stages (ages seventeen to nineteen), they develop the ability to delay gratification, think things through, compromise, express feelings verbally, and develop a greater sense of humor.

Both male and female bodies contain testosterone, with males having much more than women. While prepubescent boys and girls have about the same amount of testosterone, during puberty the average boy's testosterone production increases tenfold.[4]

During adolescence, when testosterone begins to course through a boy's veins, it virtually transforms him into a man. His voice drops, he develops muscle mass, he gains facial and body hair, and he can become more easily agitated. Testosterone also changes a boy's behavior, causing him to be more interested in attracting the attention of girls, primarily through actions such as engaging in risky behavior, competing with other males, and becoming more territorial. These behaviors seem to be cross-cultural and occur in all young males despite their environment, heritage, or race. This eagerness to engage in risky behavior is one of the reasons why young adult male mortality rates are universally higher than any other age group.

Oftentimes during puberty, your son jumps back and forth between yearning for independence and still needing the security of being taken care of by his parents. One day he feels like a full-grown man and the next he is a frightened little boy.

Teenage boys often have great levels of energy. In his book *The Wonder of Boys*, Michael Gurian talks about the powerful energy of boys:

> That energy, propelled by testosterone, and guided by the specific structure and workings of the male brain structure, is the primary cause of three behavior patterns you've probably noticed in boys:
>
> 1. the search for instant or quick gratification, whether in eating quickly, jumping from activity to activity, or quick sexual conquest;
> 2. the tendency to move quickly to problem-solving, even in emotionally complex experiences;
> 3. the tendency to find activities through which his body will build physical tension—like sports or other concentrated, single-task experiences—then release the tension with an "Ahhh."[5]

Given that boys have significantly greater levels of testosterone, what can you expect when this natural change begins?

Testosterone—Effects on Body and Mind

Probably no other known ingredient factors into masculinity more than the hormone testosterone. Testosterone not only changes a boy into a man physically, it also determines the way he acts, his sex drive, and maybe even what he does for a living. In fact, it impacts virtually every decision a man makes throughout his life.

Testosterone in both human and animal males builds muscle, fuels competition, and increases interest in sex. The stereotype regarding testosterone is that it is associated with violence, rage, aggression, sex, and power. While these stereotypes are not entirely true, testosterone levels *are* directly related to competitiveness, increased libido, and yearning for status in human males. In the animal world there does appear to be a direct link between higher levels of testosterone and dominant, aggressive behavior. I suspect that in earlier times when strength and aggression were valuable skills needed to survive, human males too were more aggressive. Civilized man has learned to control these base instincts.

Testosterone is the reason why young men like adventure, danger, competition, exploration, and risk. They even like destruction—males of all ages like explosions and fire power. Males like speed, testing themselves against their peers, and unrestrained power of any kind—the more the better.

Testosterone levels in males also fluctuate according to circumstances. For instance, during athletic competition, testosterone levels rise in males. During the heat of the battle, levels of testosterone can rise and fall depending on how the game is going. Higher levels have been discovered in the winners of athletic competitions and lower in the losers. In fact, even the testosterone levels of male spectators can rise or lower depending on their team's performance.[6]

Testosterone levels generally contribute to males being more confident, more decisive, bolder, and stronger, with more dynamic leadership skills. Certainly many women have these traits to some degree or another. However, males appear to have a biological compulsion toward leadership roles and being "in charge."

Emotional Changes and Challenges

From an emotional perspective, teenage boys are very fragile. You wouldn't know it to look at them by the way they act, but it is true nonetheless. The way their brain is developed is partially responsible for this. Males do not process or even understand their emotions as well as females. The female brain with its larger corpus callosum (a bundle of nerves connecting the two hemispheres of the brain) is better able to process "hard emotive data." This is emotional information that needs to cross between the hemispheres of the brain to be processed and communicated. Two other portions of a woman's brain that deal with emotions are also larger than in a male's. Gurian says, "The frontal lobes of the male brain, which handle many social and cognitive functions related to emotional relationships, develop more slowly in the male brain than in the female brain."[7]

For most of humankind's history, the female brain evolved and was equipped for taking care of children, requiring the development of emotive skills. In contrast, male brains have developed mainly for hunting and other spatial activities like building and designing. Hunting requires a process of following an object that is moving through space and then trying to strike it with another object, such as a rock, spear, or bullet. The same skills are required in sports, at which many males excel. Hence, the male hunter brain is more focused on objects and where they fit into the big picture, and not the object's emotions. For instance, the deer is seen as prey to be killed to feed his tribe. Gurian describes these differences this way:

> The male brain does not spend as much time processing the emotional core of a deer, ball, or enemy soldier as we might like. If it did spend a lot of time wondering about the emotions of the object, it would not be as efficient at fulfilling its function, which is in hunting, to gain dominance over and, through dominance, to transform the object into something useful to self and community. The female brain, on the other hand, evolved toward, not away from, processing the emotional core of the object. Constant and intensive child care (as well as hands-on care of sick, elderly, and disadvantaged) propels a brain structure to evolve toward in-depth emotive processing.[8]

Because males' primary occupations revolved around hunting, war, and other protection activities, their brains developed better spatial capacities involving enhanced dimensionality, depth perception, and distance. They were also programmed to de-emphasize emotive and verbal skills as well as become less empathetic. It is hard to kill animals for food or an enemy for protection if you care too much about them.[9]

Adolescent males have fragile egos, although they compensate for it by presenting to the world a hard shell. But don't mistake "bravado and compensatory grandiosity" for healthy self-esteem. Young males often measure self-esteem by an aggressive mask and posturing—sort of male armor. Males tend to close down emotionally during adolescence. Boys tend to be more direct and have fewer emotional ups and downs than girls have, but they suffer because of not being more in touch with their emotions.[10]

Moms frequently report that their sons (or husbands) do not talk about what is going on inside them. The truth is that many times we ourselves do not know what is happening or how we feel about a situation.

At lunch the other day, I overheard a woman about my age talking with a young man. The young man commented that he had had no contact with his father for years. The woman asked him if that made him sad. He responded, "No, not at all." But it was obvious by his countenance and body language that he was indeed in pain over the issue.

Emotions are confusing to young men and difficult to deal with. To admit that something hurts or makes him sad would give that emotion reality and make it valid. Then he would be forced to deal with it. As long as he can deny his emotions' existence, he does not have to face the struggle and pain of dealing with them.

A mom can assist her teenage son by helping him understand what emotion he is feeling and then walking him through processing that emotion. Just remember that males seldom process emotions and feelings by talking about them like females do. Especially if he is feeling hurt, humiliated, or vulnerable, he will be less than eager to talk about those feelings.

You can however use other methods such as object lessons or examples through movies or other remote situations. For example, if a male actor goes through a significant emotional trauma in a movie, discussing it with your son can help him understand his own emotions better. Also talking about *your* feelings and experiences in similar situations can validate and help him process his emotions as well. We will explore a boy's emotional life further in chapter 6.

Because males are more closed off from their emotions and do not show them on the surface, we tend to think they are not as emotionally sensitive or do not have feelings as deep as females. On the contrary, while males may not express their pain or vulnerability as openly as females, they are nonetheless just as wounded, if not more so, by attacks to their psyche. Perhaps the inability to articulate their feelings even contributes to the severity of the wound. Know that even though they slough off insults, jokes at their expense, bullying, and failures, they are deeply affected by them—even if they won't talk about them.

Likely the best way to help a male overcome these psychological and emotional wounds is to encourage and help him to succeed at something that he values. A boy who is made fun of because he cannot hit a baseball soon forgets all about that wound the first time he drills a home run off his offender. Because boys are physical creatures, the act of excelling at something physical in nature is redemptive to their psyche.

Psychological and Mental Changes

Many parents, with the encouragement of our culture, think that teenagers are just young adults, capable of making informed and intelligent decisions on their own. While late adolescence is a time to help them develop these skills, the truth is that the decision-making part of the brain—the prefrontal cortex—is not fully developed in individuals until about their mid-twenties. The prefrontal cortex is the part of the brain responsible for reasoning, critical thinking skills, impulse control, and sound judgment. So when we send our young people off to college at age eighteen and expect them to make good decisions, we may have unrealistic expectations. Truthfully, even if they want to make good choices, they may not have the capability. That doesn't excuse them for making bad choices; it only provides a possible explanation.

Additionally, teens are developing critical thinking skills and understanding concepts they previously did not comprehend. They grow cognitively with the ability to grasp abstract thoughts, think into the future, and develop moral reasoning. My son went through a legalistic, argumentative stage while he was developing his abstract intelligence. Sometimes—no, most of the time—it drove me crazy!

During adolescence, drastic mental development and changes are taking place with your teenage son as well. He often won't understand why he is acting the way he is. He may be more easily agitated as his levels of testosterone fluctuate. He needs to be taught to control these aggressive impulses. For instance, he might have a penchant to explode over some simple little issue. At other times he might become anxious, aggravated, or impatient with himself and others. He can be more easily angered for reasons even he may not know. He might raise his voice inappropriately or yell loudly when expressing himself just because it feels good to do so. The thrill and rush of adrenaline he receives from flexing the power testosterone gives him feels good and can become addicting if not controlled.

As my son entered adolescence, he occasionally became loud, upset, and tried to enforce his will upon others (specifically the women) in the household. I had to explain to him the physical effects of testosterone flooding his body. I explained to him that, while difficult, a man has to learn how to control these impulses and emotional outbursts for the sake of himself and others. As concentrations of testosterone level off, it becomes easier to control these impulses. Whenever he exhibited these behaviors from then on, often a look was enough to remind him of the cause and his responsibility.

Your son will also be self-conscious during this stage about everything he does. In fact, he will have an imaginary audience, thinking everyone in the world is looking at him and thinking about him. He will worry about whether he is normal or not. It is part of the self-focused world of teenagers where they are the center of the universe.

However, even though this is a time of being consumed with themselves as the center of the universe, it is also a time of recognizing new horizons. As your son's mental acumen grows, he will start thinking in more abstract concepts. His vision of the world will expand and he will begin to see a bigger picture. As he gets older, his identity and emotions will stabilize; he will look for serious relationships and will become more self-reliant.

This is a great time to allow him to grow on the inside as much as he is on the outside. Under the protective umbrella of your wisdom and control, he can experiment with making choices and understanding their consequences, learn critical thinking skills, and develop character from trial and error that might otherwise be devastating and life altering in a less protective environment. But this requires that you allow him to make his own decisions and then suffer the consequences of those choices so that he can learn from them. It also requires guiding him to learn how to use critical thinking skills to make important life choices instead of being controlled solely by his emotions and feelings. Because females tend to be more intuitive and emotion based, it is important to recognize that your feminine influence needs to be tempered by a male's more linear and logical processing style. Boys who grow up to be men who make decisions and face life from a feminized perspective (primarily using feelings instead of principles to make decisions) do not tend to fare very well. On the other hand, your influence of healing, loving, caring, compassionate, and vulnerable nurturing helps him develop into a whole, healthy, complete person.

Body Changes and Challenges (Physiological)

Okay, so what can you realistically expect to happen to your son as he enters adolescence and the teenage years? What kinds of little idiosyncratic or peculiar behaviors can Mom expect from her son during this time?

First, he will initially be very awkward and self-conscious of the changes that are taking place in his body and mind. He will likely be clumsy as his body rushes to catch up with the rapid growth happening. He will not have control of his newly gained strength and may not understand how to do things he formerly mastered. Initially, his hand-eye coordination may suffer as he learns to reprogram his mind and body interaction. He will often trip over his oversized feet, drop items, or bump into things unintentionally. His brain synapses and neurotransmitters are firing, and dendrites are growing and developing in an attempt to reprogram

37

information to coordinate with his rapid body growth and the changes taking place.

Physically his body is going through huge changes as it is flooded with testosterone. Some of these changes are embarrassing or challenging to deal with. Teenage boys get erections several times a day whether they want to or not. These erections are frequently painful in their exuberance. All too often these erections occur during the most inopportune situations or embarrassing circumstances. Many a young man knows the burning humiliation of being asked to stand up in class and having to decline or hold a book in front of his lap.

If you thought your son smelled a little funny or even downright stinky as a boy, just wait. Teen boys often become odiferous as testosterone floods their bodies. I think testosterone itself has an odor. You can almost smell the odor of raw testosterone in locker rooms as it gets sweated out of young male bodies. Expect his armpits, feet, and even his breath to start smelling stronger. It is important on many levels for young men to learn good hygiene habits at this stage in life, even though they might resist. They might not realize they now smell riper and need to step up their cleaning habits. Staying clean helps alleviate odors that could be embarrassing to them socially, causing them to feel self-conscious. Certainly, young women are not generally impressed with smelly male bodies. Since young women are pretty much all young men think about, a wise mom might be able to use this information to persuade her son to shower and wear clean clothes more often. Daily cleansing also helps eliminate the excess oil on the skin that is produced during adolescence and contributes to acne—again a symptom that can affect his self-image. Developing good health habits also speaks to the world about who he is and what he thinks is important. I've told my son and daughter that you can tell a lot about a man's character by how clean he keeps his car and what his grooming habits are like.

Next, expect your food bill to increase substantially. Especially if your son is burning extra calories through sports or other physical activities, he will consume copious quantities of groceries. Regardless, the growth of muscles, bones, and tissue, as well as the mental, psychological, and emotional development, all require a higher caloric intake. If you have more than one teenage boy in the house, expect your food bill to be one of your major monthly expenses. Adolescent boys have a tendency to "graze" all day long, and it is not unusual for them to be "hungry" even after having just eaten a large meal. These physical growth spurts require fuel on a continual basis.

The changes taking place in your son's body give him great amounts of energy in bursts but then require he sleep until noon. Make sure that your son gets plenty of physical exercise to burn off that energy but also that he gets enough sleep. Most teenagers do not get the sleep they need to be healthy.

And if you haven't noticed by now, boys just require more space in general than females. Not only do they take up more volume while sitting, but they also require more space in order to move around. Their frenzied level of energy and physicality can sometimes be exhausting to Mom. Had Theodore Roosevelt Jr., one of the greatest men in the history of our country, grown up today, he would have probably been diagnosed with Attention Deficit Hyperactivity Disorder (ADHD) and medicated as a boy. His biography often mentions his abnormally abundant energy and how his hyperactive liveliness was a trial to his mother.[11] Yet this almost frenetic degree of energy fueled a brilliant mind that absorbed everything about the world around him with a voracious appetite for knowledge. It contributed to him developing into a man who changed the world for the better.

Thankfully, Teddy's mother and father fed his voracious appetite for knowledge and new experiences instead of stifling them. The changes your son is going through during this portion of his life will also expose his passions, strengths, and weaknesses, as well as his God-given gifts. Use your powerful female intuitive abilities to recognize and help nurture these areas, and your son too will become a man who others look up to.

In summary, if you think your son is weird or abnormal, he's probably really just a normal teenager. All of these changes taking place within your son can be confusing to him and to a mother. While moms typically understand what is happening to a girl when she becomes a woman, few understand the boy-to-man journey. Now that you know the changes taking place in your son, let's discuss how best to communicate with him. Effective communication will get you through some of the difficulties that lie ahead and will give you the foundation and the tools to help him develop into a great man.

Questions for Reflection and Discussion

1. If your son has not yet started puberty, what are you doing to prepare him for the changes he will face?

2. What physical changes have you noticed in your son as he has gotten older?

3. What are the positive and negative effects of testosterone in males?

4. What is the strangest thing you have ever seen your son do?

2

COMMUNICATING
WITH TEEN BOYS

Speaking His Language

There's nothing wrong with teenagers that reasoning with them won't aggravate.

Unknown

WHILE PARENTING OUR kids during the teenage years certainly had its challenges, I actually enjoyed them. I felt I could finally communicate with them on a level that we both could understand. I also enjoyed watching them develop critical thinking skills and problem solving strategies, recognize the consequences to their actions and choices, and find passions that will remain with them for the rest of their lives. I think oftentimes teenagers are unfairly typecast as out-of-control, mercurial, hormonal monsters. I believe they get too much criticism and not enough praise. And I think, in our culture, our expectations for teenagers are too low.

That being said, living with teens can be like being strapped in an out-of-control roller-coaster ride. That's where effective communication comes in handy. For moms, learning how best to communicate with boys (especially as they are becoming men) can be a challenge. In his mind, she is now no longer as much an authority figure as she is a separate species of human being that lives in the same household. But with her superior verbal and intuitive communication skills, once a woman understands how males think, process information, and communicate, she can develop strategies to overcome these challenges.

Talking to a boy is similar to talking to a man—there's not a whole lot of difference between the two. Unfortunately, many women try to communicate with males like they do with other women—a strategy that is guaranteed to end in frustration for both genders. And like most males, your son is not above telling you what he thinks you want to hear in order to satisfy or pacify you and get you off his back. Because males are not as polished with verbal skills, they do not place as much value on them. Perhaps this is why boys and men have a tendency not to adhere to their promises and why a male's actions always speak louder than his words. Concentrate more on observing what your son *does* rather than what he *says*.

The fast-paced world of today with its sound-bite media, video games, and short video clips has atrophied many males' attention spans. Not only that, but it has narrowed our worldview into what can only be comprehended in a seven-second blurb. Books are written to have brief, simple, uncomplicated sentences, short paragraphs, with not too many concepts—after all, we are competing with a multitude of venues all vying for our attention. People do not have the time to sit in contemplation, digesting and mulling over a single sentence or paragraph for hours as we used to. This makes communicating with one another just that much more difficult.

Here are some simple tips for more effectively communicating with your teenage son (and maybe your husband too).

Communicating with Males

Researchers say up to 93 percent of all communication is through gestures, facial expressions, and body movement, instead of through words.[1] Women are much more adapted to intuitively pick up on these nonverbal cues, giving them a big advantage. It's why sons think moms can read their minds. Some women even resort to "reverse lying" or asking questions that they already know the answers to—similar to attorneys. Women seem to have the ability to think several steps ahead during a conversation, manipulating it in an almost Machiavellian way. It's no wonder boys are reluctant to verbally joust with Mom.

Females have a big advantage in that their interpersonal communication skills are so much better than the average male's are. Biologically, males have developed skills that allow them to sit and focus intensely and quietly for long periods. They are also attracted to quick-moving objects and other visual stimuli—this is one reason video games are so attractive to boys. These skills are valuable traits to have while hunting. Since that is what males did for thousands of years, it makes sense that they are biologically programmed that way. However, their verbal skills have suffered, as they are not as well developed as the average female's are.

Boys tend to develop the left side of the brain faster than girls, which leads to better visual-spatial-logical skills, perceptual skills, math skills, problem solving, building skills, and puzzle solving skills. Females hear better, see better, have a better sense of smell and touch, and are able to read emotions on a person's face more easily than males. This gives a woman a big advantage with interpersonal communication because she can pick up on nonverbal cues much more readily than a male. Males think of it as mind reading, but really females are just picking up on external clues that cue them into what is going on internally. It's one reason females are so frustrated that males do not pick up on subtle hints. But males cannot read those nonverbal clues as readily as females can.

As mentioned earlier, the corpus callosum is a bundle of nerves that connect the left and right hemispheres of the brain. A female has a larger corpus callosum than a male. This allows the two hemispheres of her brain to function better together and communicate back and forth more easily than a male's. Magnetic Resonance Imaging (MRI) and other brain-scanning studies have shown that during verbal communication, oftentimes both hemispheres of a woman's brain light up at the same time. When she stops talking, usually one hemisphere or the other will stay "lit," indicating brain wave activity. Conversely, when men speak, typically only one side or the other of their brain will light up. When they stop talking, both sides generally go blank.

Remember all those times you've asked your son, husband, or boyfriend what he's thinking and he says, "Nothing"? He was probably telling the truth. We males have the unremarkable ability to shut off our brains and just "be." It often happens when we zone out watching television, especially during commercials, or when driving the car. If you've ever had to sit quietly for long periods of time while hunting, you understand that this is a good ability to have.

Beyond that, most of the time males are not paying attention or just might not be listening, especially if they are not interested. One young woman told me her husband had gone to the doctor to have his hearing checked after the wife had complained that he wasn't listening. The doctor told him that his wife's voice was of such a pitch that he literally could not hear it (at least, that's the story he reported back to her). She earnestly wanted to know if I had ever heard of that diagnosis before in males. I didn't have the heart to tell her that either the doctor or her husband was pulling a fast one on her. It's possible, I suppose, for that to be true, but it sounds more like a husband who has come up with an ingenious story and is sticking with it.

However, males really don't hear as much as females do. Females of all ages are often frustrated that boys and men don't listen to them. But there are biological reasons for this. Michael Gurian explains it this way:

> This begins from the very beginning of life, in the brain. Males in general hear in one ear better than the other. Females in general hear more data and hear equally well in both ears. All the way through life, males hear less than females say, which creates profound problems in relationships. Boys from very early on are reported to ignore voices, even parents' voices, more than girls do. In some cases they are simply not hearing. . . . This is one of the reasons parents and anyone around a boy often report having to speak more loudly to the boy than a girl.[2]

One way to compensate for this deficiency is to address a sense that he is more skilled with. Males are generally very visual, and if you can reach out to him through that sense, you can usually acquire and retain his attention much better.

Women also generally have a much larger vocabulary than the average male and typically use about two to three times as many words each day as men do. Much of the language males use consists of grunts and other noises that sound like they come from a wounded steer. As amazing as this is to me, women *like* to talk—they actually enjoy it! They talk to process information and their feelings. They talk with each other to be closer and more intimate.

Males do things (physical activities) together to be close and develop more intimacy. When I am with my buddies or my son, we are *doing* things, not *talking* about them. Boys play together and roughhouse. If I were to just sit around and talk to someone, it would feel like I was seeing a counselor. Hence, males are often uncomfortable with too much verbal communication. Since it takes males longer to process what's being said and how we feel about it, too much information can overload our circuitry, causing us to shut down in midconversation. You can frequently see that happen while talking with your son. When he starts looking around at areas behind you or stares at the ground, you know you are losing him and it's time to stop the conversation for a while to let him get caught up.

While some eye contact is a normal part of everyday conversation, forcing him to make continuous eye contact is not an effective way of ensuring he is listening to you. Especially during emotional discussions, a male's brain will actually shut down if he is staring into the eye of a woman for too long. I cringe when I see a female teacher

47

reprimanding a boy to pay attention by repeatedly demanding he look her in the eye while she lectures him. She is actually ensuring that he will not be able to process what is being said to him. While it is important to initially get his attention visually, too much eye contact is intimidating to most males. If intimidating the boy is the objective of the conversation, then I guess those teachers are reaching their goal.[3]

All this leads many males to feel at a big disadvantage when communicating verbally. It can be quite intimidating for a male (young or old) to sit face-to-face with someone who is so much more skilled at this attribute than he is. I can remember telling my wife more than once, "Just because you can express yourself better than I can does not mean you are always right." Of course she usually *was* right, but it was frustrating nonetheless.

Males also tend not to be able to articulate their feelings very well. In fact, emotions in general are not something that most men are comfortable dealing with or can even readily identify. Males are awkward and embarrassed in emotional situations (ever watch a male stumble around when a woman is crying—or worse, another man?). Men (and boys) have to think about their feelings before they verbalize them. Women can talk, feel, and think all at the same time. If you need to discuss an emotional topic with your son, make sure you give him plenty of time to process his feelings. This may mean having several partial conversations about a topic a number of days apart. Women tend to want to talk a problem through to a solution before stopping, but sometimes this might not be possible for a male.

The following are some suggestions to help you communicate better with your teenage son (and maybe your husband as well).

48

Simple Is Better

One of the things moms need to remember is that they are so much more adept at verbal communication than the average male. It can be quite intimidating for a young male to be at such a disadvantage, especially to a female. Males do not like to feel inadequate, incompetent, or controlled. Most of the time a mom can avoid creating those feelings when talking with her son if she keeps the conversation simple. Yes, your brain easily processes emotions and information by talking about them, but your son loses focus if you give him too many details or too much information.

Learn to simplify the conversation. If you talk to your son like you do your girlfriends, he will just stop listening. Your brain is capable of processing everything taking place in the world around you, but male brains are wired to think about one thing at a time.

Every year, our ministry hosts an annual Single Mom's Family Camp. We bring about twenty-five single mothers and their children to a free three-day camp. During the camp our male volunteers play with the children during the day while I and other speakers provide education, insight, and spiritual development during classes for the moms.

At our most recent Single Mom's Family Camp, we had many more teenage boys attend than was usual in past years. One of our male mentor volunteers, Jon, was in charge of the teen boys group and related on a deep level with them. By the time camp was over, they were hanging on every word he said, seeking to gain wisdom from a man on how to be a man. They listened, enamored, as he told them secrets from a lifetime of experience as a man. He taught them how to use a pocketknife, catch and clean a fish, and build a birdhouse with their own two hands.

Jon's wife, Susan, also helped at camp. Susan (who with Jon has raised three lovely daughters) told a story of how the camp had impacted her. She told about seeing Jon at the river with the group of teen boys. As they started to leave, two of the teen boys said they did not want to go and weren't leaving. Jon slowly drawled, "Well, that's your choice. But it is against the rules of the camp for you to be here by yourself. If you choose to stay at the river by yourselves, you and your moms will probably be asked to leave the camp."

With that, Jon turned and calmly started walking up the trail away from the river with the rest of the group. The boys looked at one another, shrugged, and followed him up the trail.

Susan said what was stunning to her was that if a woman (a mom) had been in Jon's situation, she would have spent twenty minutes discussing the boys' feelings as to why they didn't want to leave and still would have never resolved the issue. She was shocked that Jon's communication method worked so well with the boys.

Jon was successful because he did two important things when communicating with teenage boys. He kept his sentences short and to the point. And he gave them options. Teen boys need to feel like they have decision-making capabilities and some control over their life. If you back them in a corner with no choices, they will likely rebel. If Jon had *ordered* them to leave, they might have challenged him just to see what would happen. They might have eventually complied but would have been angry and resentful for the rest of the camp. Giving them the option to choose allowed them to feel like adults and in control of their circumstances.

Now, it is important to understand that the choices we give teenagers are all choices we want to happen. I noticed many times when my kids were teenagers that if I gave them two or three choices in a situation, even if they were choices that favored my desired outcome, they were much more willing to acquiesce and settle for a solution that was positive. You'll notice none of Jon's choices for them were to stay at the river with no consequences. He gave them choices that guaranteed to lead to a solution that *he* wanted to end up with, while still allowing them the final say.

Speak Plainly

In *That's My Son* I encouraged moms to speak in sound-bite–type sentences to their sons. This allows them to easily process what is said to them. It takes males much longer to process information, especially if it is of an emotional nature. Many boys struggle in school because teachers do not allow them enough time to process what is being said to them before moving on to a new topic. If you need to have a longer conversation with him, engage him in a physical activity. Males process information more easily when moving, and it takes away the pressure of having an eye-to-eye conversation.

Sticking to one topic per conversation is also a good idea. Perhaps the greatest gift my wife ever gave my son and me was to start letting us know when she was changing topics during a conversation. Prior to that, she might have talked about six to seven different topics during one conversation. I would still be trying to process the first topic and not even paying attention to those that followed. Now she says, "New topic!" and we males are able to stop processing the first topic and start paying attention to the next one.

Also, remember that males have about a thirty-second attention span. If you haven't gotten to the point by then, the computer program in their mind that is programmed to solve problems kicks in and starts looking for another problem to solve. Speak directly and get to the point of your conversation as soon as reasonably possible. When my wife launches into a long, drawn-out discussion with too many details, I have to gently try to steer her back to the point of the topic or I lose my train of thought. I have trouble keeping track of all the details she throws at me. Because females are holistic in their thinking process (everything is intertwined), those details are important to the big picture in their minds. But to a male it is all unnecessary fodder that confuses the real issue.

Boys need to know what is expected of them and how long it will take in order to more easily process information. For instance, when you want your son to do a task for you, be specific. Saying something ambiguous like "Please clean your room" leaves too much room for interpretation—his idea of clean probably being different than yours. It also does not include a time expectation. Instead, try saying, "Please put all your dirty clothes in the hamper, make your bed, and vacuum your room by five o'clock tonight." This tells him simply what you expect and when you expect it. A good strategy to keep in mind is the old Boy Scout saying, "Boys need to know the objective, know the rules, and know who's in charge."

Speak plainly to your son. Males are very poor mind readers, and for all practical purposes they aren't able to read between the lines very well either. If you hint around a subject hoping your son will get it on his own, you are setting yourself up for disappointment. Males hate trying to guess what you want, or worse, what is wrong. Tell your son upfront and directly what you want and how you feel. He doesn't need all the details and who said what.

Males are often confused by signals that women send out. One example I've noticed is that males usually only smile when they are saying something positive. However, women frequently will smile while saying something negative or even expressing anger. Women also cry when they are happy—generally something males do not do. This can be confusing to a male of any age who does not generally pick up on the subtleties and nuances of internal dialogue or social intercourse (the hidden language of women) like women do. Males tend to take things spoken at face value and do not look behind them for hidden meanings. Remember that males are literal thinkers and like to process information from point A to point B in a straight line. Women, however, like to drop subtle hints and read between the lines. But males as a rule aren't very subtle. Sometimes you need to be blunt. Asking a male if he notices anything different after you've gotten your hair cut and styled sets him up for failure. For a better approach, try asking him how your new hair style makes you look. Or even better, suggest a good answer in your question, "Don't you think my new hairstyle makes me look younger?" He knows how he's supposed to answer that question. It is difficult enough for grown men to traverse the dangerous grounds of subtlety. For boys, it is nearly impossible.

Beware of Your Tongue

There's an old Viking saying, "The worst wounds come from a woman's lips." Males of all ages are seriously wounded by ridicule, contempt, and criticism, especially from the important women in their lives (wives, girlfriends, and mothers). It is a cutting and humiliating pain. Many males feel harshly judged and misunderstood by women. When this happens, males withdraw into themselves and avoid any circumstance that might cause a reoccurrence. If your son has "tuned out" and refuses to talk, there might be things that have been spoken in the past to cause him to shut down. Women can inadvertently wound a male this way by unfavorably comparing him to his peers, telling him what and how to do a task (especially if he is responsible for the task), or laughing at or making light of his shortcomings. This can be done inadvertently by a mom, especially if done in a public setting. Even good-naturedly joking about your son's faults, if done at all, is better left to the home and a private environment.

Males cannot hear, think, process information, identify emotions, and speak all at the same time like women can. Again, it is a function of his not being designed to be able to use the two hemispheres of the brain simultaneously as proficiently as women. And so, during an argument or disagreement, he may clam up or even leave without coming to a solution. It doesn't mean he doesn't care or doesn't want to resolve the situation; men's brains literally overload and have to shut down to process their feelings. If you force them beyond this point, you will notice they often respond in anger and frustration. When over-stimulated, many males eventually just tune women out. Women complain that men do not listen, but sometimes it is just because we have been fed too much information and need a break.

Again, because as a woman you are so much more proficient verbally, you have a big advantage in arguments.

Most males do not like verbal confrontations—we know we are doomed to lose any verbal argument with a female. A woman who uses that advantage ruthlessly to win an argument no matter the cost is a great source of frustration to a male. It would be like a male physically intimidating you with his greater size every time he wanted to make a point. If you've ever experienced that, you know how scary that can be. A woman's sharp tongue can be just as scary to a male as his dominant physical strength is to her. Many boys who are intimidated by their mothers at an early age respond by being physically intimidating to their mothers when they get big enough. The respect they show their mothers during adolescence is in direct proportion to the respect their mothers have shown them verbally throughout childhood.

Good communication often creates intimacy between two people. To women, intimacy means closeness. To males, it means vulnerability. Relationships in general, and intimacy in particular, are all about taking down your defenses and leaving yourself open. That means trusting people enough to give them the power to emotionally injure you, which is absolutely contrary to a man's nature.[4] Understand that a boy (or a man) has to first trust that his mother will not use her greater verbal acumen against him before he will trust her enough to be vulnerable.

Strengths, Not Weaknesses

Men forgive easier and are more easily corrected in their behaviors with positive feedback than women are.

Dr. Laura Schlessinger,
The Proper Care and Feeding of Husbands

Another huge asset you have to positively influence and communicate with your son is to *work on his strengths, not his weaknesses.* Most segments of our culture tell us to work on our weaknesses, not our strengths. But that is a form of criticism, not encouragement. Nurturing our areas of strength is encouraging and uplifting. Women of influence nurture strengths instead of exploiting weaknesses.

It is a male's instinctive desire to win the approval and admiration of his mother and, later in life, his wife. He yearns for his woman to be proud of him. A mother who uses the qualities of admiration and respect builds a boy up instead of discouraging him. Males complain of being nagged by women, but generally women are just trying to get their needs met by engaging in that behavior. A woman who uses respect as a tool with a male can get the lawn mowed or other chores done much more easily than by constantly complaining.

In your everyday conversations with your son, be sure to lift up masculinity to a higher standard. For instance, when he asks why he has to do some chore, respond by saying, "Because that's what good men do." Likewise, you can get him to react or respond differently when he is doing something annoying by saying, "Don't do that. Men don't act that way." Be intentional about promoting healthy masculinity. All boys are eager to learn their roles as men. They want someone to tell them what a man does and how he acts. Having respect for his and all masculinity ensures that he will attempt to live up to a higher standard of behavior and feel good about his gender. Moms who are male affirming help boys enjoy how God created them.

So don't just focus on the things your son does wrong. Instead, try focusing on the things he does right rather than being overly critical of his weaknesses. Study him carefully to find out what his strengths and weaknesses are. Then help him understand his strengths—his gifts from God. Many people do not know what their strengths or weaknesses are. All of us have been blessed with certain skills and find ourselves lacking in others. Find out where he excels and help him use and cultivate those strengths to succeed in life. Encourage him to develop those gifts. When we use our God-given gifts to their potential, we lead very fulfilling lives.

A mother has a wonderful tool with her powerful communication skills. Using that power wisely can not only make your life easier, it can also help your son grow into a healthy, even a great, man.

Questions for Reflection and Discussion

1. Is your son easy to talk with? Did that change as he became an adolescent?

2. Do you agree that women have a big advantage in verbal communication over males? In what ways have you recognized that advantage?

3. Do you ever complain that your son does not "listen" to you?

4. Have you ever observed your son "shutting down" when you talk to him? Why do you think he did that?

5. Do you believe that a mom has a powerful ability to wound a boy with her tongue?

3

MOM AND SON

What Young Men Need from Mom

*My mother was the most beautiful woman I ever saw.
All I am I owe to my mother. I attribute all my success
in life to the moral, intellectual and physical education
I received from her.*

George Washington

M Y WIFE TOLD me about a dream she had when our son Frank was a teenager. "I was walking down a gravel road hand in hand with Frank. He was about three or four years old in my dream. We were having a lovely time when suddenly he started hurrying ahead, stretching our grip. He was looking back at me and, in his husky little-boy voice, saying, 'Come on, Mom! Hurry, hurry . . .'

I yelled, 'Frank! Frankie, wait, don't go so fast yet,' but he kept straining and pulling away from me, telling me to 'Hurry, come on, Mommy, come on.' Finally he broke our grip and moved away from me farther and farther until I could barely see him. In my dream I was crying so hard at losing him, not in a bad way, just that my little boy was gone. I awoke sobbing so deeply. That dream affected me for days to follow. Even now, I cry, recalling his little-boy voice and knowing I can't pick him up and swing him around, smooch his neck till he squeals, and laugh with him because we didn't have a care in the world!"

She went on to say, "The mother/son separation had firmly and securely taken place. My apron strings were cut, and at thirteen my little boy was not my little boy any longer. The childhoods of my children, while they were the most exhausting, trying, frustrating, and all-new-every-day experiences, were the best years of my life as a mom. Now, someday I hope to smooch a little grandbaby. Won't that be the next great adventure!"

A Mother's Influence

> My mother had a great deal of trouble with me, but I think she enjoyed it.
>
> Mark Twain

As a mother and parent, you and his father (if your son is one of the lucky ones having a father at home) are your son's foremost role models of a man and a woman (masculinity and femininity). You also provide the values and worldview that your child believes to be true. Your nurturing, loving guidance helps your son grow up to be a healthy, happy, and well-rounded person. You make sure the children are safe, fed properly, washed, and clean, with all their needs met. Your presence helps children thrive and grow like vigorous stalks of corn in black, fertile soil. Your nurturing instincts bring vitality to family life. Your healing touch cures everything from scraped knees to bruised egos. Your gentle compassion soothes even the most horrendous betrayal. Your son especially learns from you sensitivity, compassion, empathy, and caring for others.

We tend to believe that our influence over our children wanes as they become teenagers, but this is not true. Time and time again, studies show that parents have more influence in their kids' lives than anyone—even as teenagers! Your teenagers want to know what you believe in, what is right, what you live for, and what you think is important in life. They want to know from their parents what is true, what is wrong, and what mistakes to avoid in life (of course that doesn't always mean they will follow your advice). You are more important than any movie actor, pop singer, model, or TV star. You are more influential than newspapers, magazines, teachers, coaches, video games, or TV shows. But if we don't use that influence, it is lost forever.

Understand that whether or not we use our influence intentionally, our kids are likely to follow our example. If you live a life of promiscuity, chances are your kids will too. If you live a life of integrity, it's likely your kids will too. My parents constantly told me not to smoke cigarettes or drink alcohol, but they did both to excess and so that was the model I followed as a teenager and young adult until I discovered the folly of those actions. Wounds, abuses, and destructive behavior seem to be passed from generation to generation unless someone takes intentional steps to break them.

Not only that, but a boy's mother has a huge influence on how a boy sees himself as a man—both positively and negatively. Mothers can short-circuit the fragile connection between boyhood and manhood with their words and attitude. A mother's influence on how a boy feels about himself as a man is very significant. A mother who despises men can make life difficult for a boy. For women who have been hurt by men in their life, this can present a real challenge. Paul Coughlin says it this way: "Give him a mother who was beaten by her father. She'll do the best she can to attack burgeoning manhood in her boys. She'll look at powerful men with contempt and then use her verbal acumen to castrate young male souls. Thereby she condemns a boy's manhood: When she criticizes his father, the boy will struggle with the belief that he's the fruit of defective seed."[1]

But mothers who respect and admire healthy masculinity can make a boy believe he was created for greatness. Through her affirming power, she can lift him up to be and do things he could never become or accomplish without her powerful influence in his life.

The Influence of Women on Masculinity

> Every mother is like Moses. She does not enter the Promised Land. She prepares a world she will not see.
>
> Pope Paul VI

Women play a significant role in developing masculinity within a culture. Women in a society influence the *type* of men a culture creates in several ways. One way is by those men they choose to have sex with. Men conform to the requirements and rules to which they are held accountable. This applies to relationships just as much as to the business or sports world. Bottom line, the character of the men a woman sleeps with encourages that character in all men. If enough women have sex with men of low character, that is what all men will aspire to be like. If they sleep with only men of noble character, then that is the standard all men will strive to live up to. Either way, their offspring (male and female) will tend to follow in those footsteps. If mothers sleep with men who abuse and abandon them, their daughters will likely be attracted to men of similar character. The role model the father sets for boys is very important in how they live their life. A father who is absent or abandons his offspring is much more likely to produce a son who follows in his footsteps. Women who choose to procreate with men who abandon them leave a legacy of abandonment for their sons to follow. Likewise, a father who abuses his wife passes that legacy on to his son as well. The modeled behavior of both the mother and father influences future behavior in children of both genders. Not always—of course there are examples of people who are nothing like their parents. But more often than not, we seem to be programmed to unconsciously mimic those behaviors and make choices that lead us to end up in the role that was modeled for us.

Unfortunately, in this regard, many women are notoriously poor judges of what constitutes authentic masculinity. All you have to do is look around at all the women who have chosen men who abandoned or abused them or used them purely for their own self-gratification. Men will live up to whatever standard women set for them. Men will do what women tolerate and avoid what women will not abide. Reportedly, during the Civil War, women would hiss publicly at men who avoided military duty. When women will not tolerate cowardice, men are forced to live up to standards of higher character.[2]

The other way women influence masculinity in a culture is by how they choose to raise their sons. If women choose to raise sons without a healthy male influence in their lives (either by choice or consequence), it negatively impacts a boy's life for as long as he lives. Darwin's *theory* of evolution (italics mine) purports that in order to survive through natural selection, members of a species breed with the strongest of that species to produce superior offspring. This ensures the survival of the species. For thousands upon thousands of years, the laws of survival dictated that women chose men who were most capable in order to ensure their survival and that of their offspring. They mated with men who would stay with them, providing protection and provision, thus guaranteeing the survival of their children. Even as recently as a century ago, this natural selection process appears to have been a requirement for survival. However, for the past three decades or so, a shift has taken place where more women seem to be choosing men who abandon them, leaving them and their children to fend for themselves. What caused this shift in the decision-making process of women in our culture? In other times, women who poorly selected mates were doomed to failure. Their bloodline soon died off. Is this shift a by-product of an advanced civilization where it's easier (even encouraged) to raise children without men? Perhaps—or perhaps it is the result of generations of cycles being passed down until it has reached a critical mass where this shift is being noticed more.

A mother can influence a boy's character by the environment she raises him in. By allowing and encouraging healthy male influences, allowing him to learn by trial and error, not rescuing him to extreme, and instilling character values in him by holding him accountable—while still nurturing him—she creates a whole man who will face the world confidently. This kind of man will lead his family and contribute to the betterment of society.

What Does He Need Most from Mom Now?

Before becoming a mother I had a hundred theories on how to bring up children. Now I have seven children and only one theory: love them, especially when they least deserve to be loved.

Kate Samperi

While a mother is not as necessary in the nurturing aspect of her teen son's development as she was when her son was younger, she is still hugely important to a boy at this stage of life. A son still needs his mother's nurturing and healing touch to sooth the injustices of the world. Now that he's older, though, Mom needs to realize that she can't cradle her little boy in her arms anymore to lick his wounds. She must rely on her sixth sense to use her healing touch in ways that appeal to his burgeoning manhood.

Mom also teaches her son many valuable lessons necessary for survival in the world. Ideally, a boy or young man has both a mother and a father to model male and female roles for him. He learns from this modeled relationship how to communicate, how to interact, and even how to love a woman. In a perfect world, he learns toughness, leadership, and competency from his father and the more nurturing elements of his personality such as love, tenderness, and sensitivity from his mother. When either of these models is absent from his life, it makes it more difficult for him to develop a full range of life skills necessary to succeed as a man, husband, and father.

From his mother a boy learns many necessary traits to succeed in life. He typically learns compassion and empathy from her. He learns the value of women and of relationships. He learns about sacrifice, gentleness, caring, and unconditional love. His mother is the example of a woman, a wife, and a mother that he carries with him for his entire life.

What Does Nurturing Look Like to a Teenage Boy?

Before you were conceived I wanted you. Before you were born I loved you. Before you were here an hour I would die for you. This is the miracle of love.

Maureen Hawkins

I recently spoke to a single mom in Detroit who was trying to teach her young teenage son the character trait of chivalry. She was making him open her car door for her and hold an umbrella for her when it was raining. He thought this behavior was all somehow a bit unreasonable. After all, why should he get wet? The kicker though was when she started making him walk on the outside of the sidewalk (an old custom that was originally designed to protect women from getting mud splashed on them from carriages). He said, "That's not fair. If a car comes along, I'm the one who will get killed!" She gently explained to her son that she was teaching him chivalrous behavior and that it would benefit other people someday. That someday a young lady would turn his head and he would be her knight in shining armor.

Five Tips on Ways to Get Boys (and Men) Excited about Living like a Gentleman

1. Nearly all males are motivated by one of two things—sex or food. Acting like mannerly gentlemen can help them achieve either of those two goals (the first hopefully deferred if they are single). Males who know this are quickly encouraged to behave like gentlemen.
2. Male role models who act like gentlemen produce boys and men who act like gentlemen.
3. Encourage chivalrous behavior. Always lift masculinity to a higher standard in your daily speech and interactions. Discuss the nobility of healthy masculinity.
4. Encourage your daughters to date only young gentlemen. If enough women choose only men with manners, it encourages all males to act that way. The standard that women hold men to—high or low—is the one to which men will aspire.
5. Watch movies like *Cinderella Man*—it's cool to be a gentleman.

But this mom was teaching her son much more than that. She was teaching him to respect all women. She was teaching him about his duty as a man to protect women and treat them as precious commodities, to honor and cherish them. She was teaching him the honor of sacrifice. She was teaching him that manhood is about doing for others before doing for ourselves. That is what makes a culture successful—not when men are self-focused on their own needs and wants. This young man will grow up to understand (and thus be more comfortable with) his roles as a man in life. He will use his masculine gifts to make the lives of those he loves and who are under his protection more rich and fulfilled.

This mom was actually nurturing her son by helping him become a man. Boys and young men often consider advice and training on how to successfully navigate through life to be nurturing. Boys value advice and training that help them succeed in life. Moms can play a special role in helping her son understand females and their needs, which are often confusing to a male.

Another area that a mother can help her son is by teaching him manners. This teaches him to respect himself and others. Practicing good manners will also help him get along in the world, because someone with good manners is universally liked and respected regardless of the culture.

A mom helps her son by teaching him how to talk to a female. Females are very confusing to young (and old) males. By learning how to communicate with a female, he will be at least marginally more comfortable navigating through the feminine world.

Learning how to dance properly (not today's gyrations) is important in impressing young women. Since young men spend an inordinate amount of time thinking about and trying to impress young women, this skill will be very beneficial to him as he establishes himself in the male pecking order of life.

All of these skills help to breed confidence in a young man. Young men who are confident are less apt to try to prove to themselves and to the world that they are men.

Letting Go

The mother-child relationship is paradoxical and, in a sense, tragic. It requires the most intense love on the mother's side, yet this very love must help the child grow away from the mother, and to become fully independent.

Erich Fromm

One of the biggest challenges moms tell me they face is "letting go" of their son and allowing him the freedom to become a man. Their son is their precious baby whom they are loathe to lose. Moms often fear the burden of responsibility that manhood brings with it and worry that their son will not be able to carry that burden.

Your son has been created by God to have the special ability to function and carry out his roles in life. A man has been uniquely equipped to carry the burdens of those roles. Aubrey Andelin says it this way: "When God blessed man with the responsibility to guide, protect, and provide for his family, he also blessed him with the temperament and capability to function in this role. He was given the capacity to shoulder heavy responsibility, to endure stresses and strains of the marketplace, to struggle with difficulties and make weighty decisions. Although his burdens may be heavy, and discouragement enter in, *he has the capacity to do his work.*"[3]

When a mother interferes with this process of a boy's growth to manhood by continually rescuing him or keeping him from failure and not allowing him to suffer its consequences, she is actually thwarting God's design in her son. That is how God designed boys to grow into men. Even though a boy doesn't like it, he learns nearly all of his manly qualities by failing and persevering again. When Mom protects him from life's challenges, it retards his growth toward manhood.

At some point, boys must break away from the tightly wrapped arms of motherhood in order to achieve true masculinity. They must make a break from the world of women. And men must recognize that they cannot rely on women to hand them the crown of masculinity.

I have a friend, an ex-NBA player, who grew up in the projects of an urban city. He was raised by women—a mother and three sisters. He shared with me that one of the biggest problems he faced as he became a man was that he was never taught healthy coping skills by a man. He had only female influences early in life, and so he found himself frustrated and angry in stressful situations. He had learned to make decisions based on his feelings. Because he couldn't channel his emotions properly, he made irrational choices that led to consequences like being kicked off his high school basketball team despite being an All-American and then losing a full-ride college scholarship by fighting with his coach. The problem followed him into the NBA because the players are generally surrounded by "yes-men"—no one ever tells them when they are wrong. Only by finding some strong male mentors and role models to help guide him was he able to turn his life around. Today he devotes his life to helping young men understand what it takes to be successful by giving them hope and knowledge.[4]

The more a man allows a woman (mother, wife, girlfriend) to define his masculinity, the less of a man he will be. Why? Because a woman is not a man—she cannot empower masculinity. A man has to follow his male instincts instead of following a female's direction of what a man is and what his role should entail. When I wrote *That's My Son*, our son Frank was a teenager. Frank is now a young man living on his own. But even though he's twenty-three now, his mama is still quick to want to run in and rescue him when she thinks he needs it. Frank now lives in a house with a couple of other young men. Shortly after moving in with them, he learned a valuable lesson about budgeting his money. After spending all of his money before payday, he was forced to spend about three days going hungry until he got paid. It almost killed my wife not to bring him care packages or go over and cook a meal for him. However, somehow Frank survived, and I suspect he will be much more careful about budgeting his resources in the future. It's a lesson he will not soon forget. If his mom had rescued him, he would still be spending his money on frivolous things without regard to the consequences. Because of what he learned, Frank tells me he has sworn off fast-food restaurants and has bought groceries and is cooking his own meals for the first time in his life (he called and asked for his mom's recipe for meat loaf the other day). Amazing what an empty belly will do for a fella, isn't it? But wouldn't it have been even better if he had learned that lesson *before* leaving home? We do a disservice to our young men by not teaching them early in life to suffer the consequences of their choices.

Part of the "letting go" process involves allowing your son to be tested and even pushed by another man. Because my wife was raised in a dysfunctional home, she feared that being too critical of our children would cause them to have poor self-esteem. Consequently, she was sensitive to my pushing Frank too hard. Against my better judgment, I often acquiesced to her fears. I allowed myself to be ruled by my emotions (desire to make my wife happy) instead of using principles that I knew were right. As a coach I knew better but did not provide the same leadership skills at home that I did on the basketball court. The lesson I learned I now teach all the time—that boys need to learn to make decisions using principles and not feelings. Frank will readily admit today that he wishes I would have pushed him harder to succeed and perform up to his capabilities. The flaw in my wife's concern (while valid) was that we were not a dysfunctional family. My expectations would not have been unhealthy, causing lowered self-esteem,

Tips for Helping Your Son Develop

- Praise him every day (for legitimate reasons—not just undeserved praise).
- Include him in the decision-making process of the family.
- Give him reasons <u>why</u> when you tell him to do something. Tell him why before he asks.
- Encourage him to read. Readers are leaders. (Theodore Roosevelt and other great leaders throughout history were voracious readers. Encourage young men to read things that interest them. For instance, Robert E. Howard's works with his characters like the Cimmerian hero Conan or prizefighting "Sailor Steve Costigan" are excellent adventures with well-written prose. Even Howard's poetry is manly and inspiring or, as H. P. Lovecraft called it, "weird, warlike, and adventurous.")[5]
- Pray <u>with</u> him and <u>for</u> him every day (he needs to see you and his father in prayer together).

but would have in fact been healthy and actually caused growth and good self-image because of his success. Obviously, there are unhealthy levels of expectations that we can place on our sons (we've all seen "Little League Dad" who screams at his son during baseball games), but low expectations of boys may be just as bad or worse. When men are not allowed to push boys beyond their self-limiting boundaries, it is unhealthy for them in their development toward becoming a healthy man.

Iron ore is a chemical element found in the earth's crust. Iron, while tough and hard, rusts easily and has limited uses. Steel is iron that has been forged through a smelting process to make it tough and unbreakable. Steel is formed by treating molten (melted) iron with intense heat and mixing it with carbon. Steel is harder and stronger than iron. If it did not undergo high levels of heat and pressure, it would be brittle and break easily. Steel is rust-resistant, readily recycled, and can be more easily welded. The ability to efficiently make steel from iron rapidly advanced civilization. Steel is used to make most of the things we rely on in our world such as machines, cars, tools, knives, appliances, ships, airplanes, trains, and many other things. The intense heat and pressure it undergoes take a material that is already hard and strong and make it an even more useful tool that benefits everyone on our planet. Without that "smelting" process, neither iron nor young males would be made into a better material that benefits the world. Boys need men to "forge" them into hardened steel that their families and our society can depend upon.

A Female Role Model

> Her dignity consists of being unknown to the world; her glory is in the esteem of her husband; her pleasures in the happiness of her family.
>
> Jean Rousseau

The evil one seems to have a special hatred for females. One of his greatest weapons against women seems to be words. He first deceived Eve in the Garden of Eden by whispering lies in her ear. He continues to deceive women today by whispering in their ears lies that prey upon their most vulnerable areas—looks and worth. He tells a woman that she is fat, ugly, weak, unattractive, unlovable, old, unwanted, and unworthy. He then uses our culture to reinforce those lies through media messages that are guaranteed to ensure that women feel bad about their beauty, bodies, and value. These psychological attacks affect women so powerfully that they can develop eating disorders, body image distortions, and even learn to despise themselves and feel undeserving of love. Some women even believe they deserve to be physically and emotionally abused.

Women today are still susceptible to words' effect—believing flattering or deceitful words. Because of their nurturing nature, women look hard for reasons to believe what men and boys tell them. They also look for the good aspects of a male's character almost to a fault, overlooking bad traits by overemphasizing any good trait they can find.

It is important for your son that you overcome these attacks on femininity and help your son recognize the inherent value of females. He needs to learn early that women are to be honored and cherished. He needs to recognize the importance females have to the family structure, to relationships, and to a man himself. He needs to understand a female's equal status to males as human beings in God's creation. He will be less likely to learn those things from a mom who doesn't feel good about herself as a woman.

From his mom, a young man learns many things about females and how to relate to them. Females are very confusing creatures to the average young man. Moms not only provide a model of healthy female sexuality, but they provide the first and most important model of how a woman responds to a man, how she talks to him, the level of respect he deserves, the level of respect a woman deserves, a woman's role in a relationship, how a woman loves a man, and how two people can live together as husband and wife.

In addition, the role model of womanhood he observes in his mother is one that will greatly influence what he looks for in a wife. Many a young man with a broken mother married a damsel in distress hoping to rescue her.

Unfortunately, men can seldom rescue and heal a broken woman—only God can.

As a mom, you are the most important female in your son's life until he takes a wife. Your preparation with him and role model for him determines not only the kind of woman he marries but to some degree his success as a husband and a man. Never underestimate your value in his life.

Connecting with Your Son

The one thing I hear from most moms is that they have trouble connecting with and understanding their son. They want a close relationship and they want to be an important part of his life, but somehow boys at this age seem to be a conundrum. Moms say stuff like, "How can I connect with my teenage son?" or "My son is so different from my daughter, I just don't understand him."

So how does a mom make a connection with her son at this critical time of life? It's not like you can sit down and have a heart-to-heart chat with him like you do your girlfriend. Author and friend Julie Barnhill told me about the challenge of connecting with her second son and how different he is from her firstborn son:

> As for Mom and teenage boy . . . *sigh* . . . where do I begin?!
> Son #2 is incredibly different than his older brother (the Marine.) Believe it or not, Marine man-child is sensitive, talkative, and very in touch with expressing his emotions. Son #2, eh, not so much. Has a lot to prove to himself (and I think to us, in his mind). He's a much harder nut to crack, and I've had to work a lot harder to find a connecting point with him than I did his older brother. We're actually doing a workshop together in March regarding

a mom interpreting the language of the teenage boy. I'm trying to find avenues to connect with him. I watch UFC with him in an effort to connect. I think time spent with him watching The Military Channel's show, *Special Ops*, is about as good as it gets as a mom of a teenage son.

I think Julie is on to something important. Finding activities he enjoys that you can do together with your son is very important in connecting with him. Many of those interests will involve physical activities. Males develop intimacy by doing things with each other, and males like companionship. If you can find even a couple of activities you can do together without being intrusive (don't make him shoot hoops with you when the guys are waiting for him), you can connect with him. When our oldest child entered middle school, we put a big swimming pool in the backyard with a large trampoline next to it. We wanted a physical activity that we could do together as a family and one that would prompt their friends to spend time at our home. Even though it was expensive to maintain and Oregon isn't the best state for outdoor swimming most of the year, we thought it was worth the investment.

Additionally, I've never seen a young man who didn't like food. Many moms can maintain a connection by using food as a catalyst. Any time our son had friends over, we always tried to feed them, even if it was just pizza. They never once turned us down no matter the time of day. This served the purpose of having our son home more as his friends always wanted to be at our house. By being home more often, it allowed us to play a bigger role in influencing him and monitoring the friends in his life.

Find ways to connect with your son and your powerful influence as a mother will pay huge dividends.

Questions for Reflection and Discussion

1. Have you realized yet that you will need to start "cutting the apron strings" with your son? Why is this necessary in the development of a male?

2. In what ways are mothers influential both positively or negatively in the lives of boys?

3. What impact do women have on masculinity in a culture?

4. What three things do you think your son needs most from his mother?

4

DAD AND SON

What Young Men Need from Dad

Papa's missing. Things are falling apart because Papa's gone. If Papa were here, he'd fix it.

Lucille Ball, shortly before her death,
when asked why families in America were falling apart

THERE IS AN old legend regarding the Cherokee Indian youth's rite of passage. When a boy is ready to become a man, the father takes his son into the forest, blindfolds him, and leaves him alone. He is required to sit on a tree stump the entire night and not remove the blindfold until the rays of the morning sun shine through it. He cannot cry out for help to anyone. After he survives the night, he is considered a man. He cannot tell the other boys of this experience, because each boy must come into manhood on his own.

The boy is naturally terrified. He can hear all kinds of noises. Wild beasts must surely be all around him. Maybe even humans who might do him harm.

During one boy's ordeal, the wind blew the grass and earth and shook his stump, but he sat stoically, never removing the blindfold. It was the only way he could become a man! Finally, after a horrific night the sun appeared and he removed his blindfold. It was then that he discovered his father sitting on the stump next to him. He had been at watch the entire night, protecting his son from harm.

This story is a perfect illustration of how a father protects and guides his son. His protection is proactive but often in the background where it cannot be seen. As men we are frequently called upon to use our long-range vision, discernment, and experience to protect those we love without them even knowing what is happening. It is how men teach and guide our protégés and those we love. And teaching and guidance about life from a father is very often how boys spell love.

Boys need to start getting hardened for life by their fathers and other older men. Life is tough. Boys who enter life "soft" are at a big disadvantage in trying to succeed in life and lead their families. Many boys suffer because more often in our culture women lead their families, either by choice or default. Some men refuse to lead their families, and so Mom has no choice—someone has to be in charge. Single mothers have no choice but to be leaders of the home. But frequently, especially in blended families, if the father is not biologically related to the son, Mom either controls or interferes in the discipline and decision-making role. This interference cripples the stepfather's influence and causes the boy to lose respect for him. And frankly, sometimes women grab control of the home and do not let their husbands be the leaders they secretly wish they were.

The Power God Gave Fathers

One father is more than one hundred school masters.

George Herbert

One way to judge the degree of power or influence that something has is to observe what happens when it is absent. God has given men, especially fathers, tremendous power to influence the lives of those around them. The lives of women and children in particular are hugely impacted by what a man does or doesn't do with his life. For instance, men who are good fathers and husbands mightily bless the lives of their wives and children. Those men who are absent, abusive, or unconnected have just as big of a negative influence in the lives of their families. For a boy, his father is *the* most important role model in his life.

In the biographical movie of Johnny Cash's life, *Walk the Line*, Cash is haunted by his inability to get his father's approval and blessing. He is driven to accomplish more and more, buying bigger and better material items in an attempt to win his father's pride. He eventually turns to drugs to deaden the wound in his heart from his father's scorn and contempt. His life spirals out of control until he eventually loses everything.

Men have been given tremendous power to be able to impact people's lives—for good or bad—by the things they do or don't do. Most men I know either don't recognize or don't understand this power. When I speak at conferences on the tremendous power men have, men are always surprised and somewhat shocked. I suspect it is because our culture never tells them of this life-changing energy God bestowed upon us. In fact, just the opposite, our society (movies, television, commercials, etc.) seems to go out of its way to destroy and belittle masculinity.

Like anything with great power, masculinity has the potential for life or for death. It all depends on how and why it is used. Our culture fears the potential negative effects of masculine power and so tries to squelch it before it reaches its potential. Masculinity gone awry has destroyed many lives and damaged many who are helpless and defenseless in our world. Perhaps this fear of the power of masculinity causes many to try to diminish it instead of nurturing it to its full positive potential, to cage it so it cannot cause harm. If we (especially men) do not train boys how to be good men, we shouldn't expect anything other than what we get in return.

Our Better Dads ministry works with many single moms and fatherless children. Most of this population has been devastated by the loss of masculine leadership in their lives. They are more vulnerable to be preyed upon by a variety of predators, suffer from poverty, and have a much higher propensity to exhibit other at-risk behaviors such as substance abuse, sexual promiscuity, and criminal activities. Children from single-parent homes are far more likely to do significantly more poorly in every measurable educational outcome than children from intact families. In addition, these behaviors are generational in nature, being passed down from one generation to the next. For instance, where generations of females in a family are all single mothers, we observe a lineage of males abandoning their families, generations of males who end up in prison, or generational addictions to drugs and alcohol.[1]

Part of our goal in our three-day Single Mom's Family Camp is to begin a process to break generational cycles. We do this through education and mentoring. We provide volunteer adult male role models to play with the kids in activities like soccer, basketball, BMX biking, rock wall climbing, fishing, swimming, tubing, and hiking. All the while, I and other powerful speakers work with the moms teaching them life skills, relationship and parenting development, and spiritual enrichment. Our female volunteers then pamper the moms with a "Spa Day," including desserts and prayerful gifts like foot washings, pedicures, manicures, and massages. They also get a karaoke ladies night out! It is a time of blessing, honoring, healing, and spiritual reconnection for many of them.

Each of these women and children suffers mightily because of the lack of positive males in their lives. The boys and girls blossom under the love, guidance, and discipline of positive masculinity—some for the first time in their lives! We see positive behavioral changes almost immediately. Within a short period of time, the kids become calmer, more polite, and eager to have fun. The boys especially bloom under masculine guidance. You can see their self-esteem grow as the men teach them basic skills. We even had a few adult male mentors who grew up without fathers who have benefitted from learning these skills! The teen boys practically hang on every word spoken by the men as they impart practical wisdom and insight on everyday living. And the yearning for healthy masculine affection is evident. Their "father hunger" is almost palpable. Around the campfire I watch as previously unruly and angry little boys crawl up onto the laps of the men and nestle into their chests, contentedly gazing into the fire for hours, sucking up that "masculine essence" they crave like dry sponges.

One grandmother attendee reported to me with pride that her sixteen-year-old grandson had recently defended her from the unwanted attentions of another man. Her grandson was without a positive older male in his life to teach this to him, and she attributed his unexpected behavior to what he had learned listening to my workshop CDs and at the Single Mom's Family Camp they had recently attended. She went on to say, "I started to cry when he did that. It was the first time in my entire life that a man had defended me, and it felt so different from anything I had ever experienced before."

Another single mom who attended the camp commented to my wife that she was very nervous sitting next to me, as she had never sat next to a "good" man before.

Can you imagine going through your entire life as a woman never having been defended by a man before or even having sat next to a good man? It is almost incomprehensible to me. I think we take for granted many of the things that this population of lost "widows and orphans" desperately needs and wants.

Every boy needs to hear his father say two things: *I love you* and *I'm proud of you*. Without that blessing, a man will search for it and try to earn it throughout his lifetime. God granted men and fathers a magnificent power to positively impact the lives of his own wife and children, but even more so, the lives of other women and children as well. It is a power that a man can choose to use, choose not to use, or choose to abuse. Whatever he chooses, with great power comes great responsibility.

When I speak at Promise Keepers Canada events, I frequently discuss healing the father wound. After talking about the power of fathers to impact our lives and the necessity to heal those father wounds in order to move forward and become healthy fathers and men, I give an altar call. Men rush down to the front, many in tears and sobbing, desperately seeking the prayers of other men to ask God to heal those lifelong wounds. Fatherless boys are surrounded by older men praying for them as they cry out for a father to hold them. Even elderly men are among those weeping and looking for relief and forgiveness. Their wounds are deep and shocking and something you don't soon forget. It is an awesome testament to the power that God has given fathers.

What Happens to Boys without Dad?

Several years ago we began presenting seminars for women on raising boys to become good men.[2] The seminars are for mothers, grandmothers, aunts, teachers and administrators, social workers, and any other women who work or live with boys. But we found a huge segment of our culture where women were being forced to raise sons on their own and were desperate to understand what their sons needed to grow into good men. Many of these women faced big disadvantages raising boys and understanding what their sons needed not only by not being male themselves but also by not having been raised with a father or brothers while growing up. After presenting enough of these seminars, it became clear that one of the biggest challenges these moms faced was not having positive male role models available in their sons' lives.

In response to this dilemma, we started a program called Standing Tall. Standing Tall is a mentoring program for fatherless boys, similar to a faith-based Big Brothers program. It originally started in partnership with a local Bible college. There we trained male seminary students to spend a couple of hours a week with fatherless boys identified through our seminars for moms. Almost immediately we started seeing some startling results. Mothers of the boys began reporting changes in their sons' entire countenances. Their sons were better behaved, less angry, more respectful of them, and doing better in school. Some credited the presence of the mentors with their sons' improvement in reading scores (even though they never read together). They noted behavioral changes such as cessation of bedwetting. Nearly all of the boys experienced more self-confidence and composure during their daily life activities.

We teach the mentors to use physical activities with the boys. Many fatherless boys spend large amounts of unsupervised time in front of the television or video games, which is unhealthy on so many levels. We encourage mentors to proactively use "teaching" opportunities. We encourage them to teach things such as how to drive a nail, catch a baseball, shoot basketball hoops, ride a bike, use a pocketknife safely, hike in the wilderness, and so forth—all the things that boys without dads do not learn and without which they feel inadequate. We sometimes teach older boys skills such as shaving and other appropriate personal hygiene tips. You might be surprised at the simplest things you or I take for granted that fatherless boys do not know how to do. And because it is embarrassing to ask, they often stumble through life without ever getting that knowledge.

We encourage the mentors to intentionally teach character traits such as self-discipline, perseverance (not quitting), honesty, courage, respect for women (mother) and others. Many of these boys do not learn these character traits, not because the mother doesn't value them, but because they are more readily learned and accepted coming from another older male.

Another issue we observe in fatherless boys is the unwillingness to accept challenges. Because they have no confidence and a reluctance to experience humiliation through their failures, many of these boys do not receive the valuable lessons and self-esteem garnered from failing and persevering until they succeed. They also become frustrated and quit anything the first time it becomes difficult. They tend to cry easier than most boys. When they fall down and scrape a knee, they will instantly cry and wait for Mom to come rescue them. If a man picks them up and dusts them off, they recognize they are not really hurt and stop crying right away. Again a male's presence helps to guide and encourage them to persevere until they succeed, thereby gaining the positive self-image and confidence to accept risk and attempt challenges in other areas of life.

Very often they have been feminized by having only female influences in their lives. They observe only a feminine outlook on how to respond to life. They come to expect to be "rescued" by Mom (or another female) and frequently will not try new things. In fairness to them, they don't know any better—Mom has always rescued them. As they become older, they get indecisive, passive, docile, and unable to commit to a relationship. They tend to rely on females to make all the decisions that govern their lives and seldom take on natural leadership roles.

These boys are also often angry. Sometimes their anger is externalized and apparent in social and educational venues, and other times it is internalized into passive-aggressive behavior. Frankly they have a right to be angry—they have been deprived of their God-given right to a father to teach them how to make their way in this big, harsh world. They do not have a father to teach them, protect them, and empathize with their struggles. Frequently, though, this anger is being used to cover other emotions such as fear, humiliation, anxiety, vulnerability, or even pain. Unless these boys are taught to recognize this, they are doomed to believe they can solve any problem in life using anger and other unhealthy coping mechanisms.

Another observation we make in fatherless boys is the propensity they all have to be somewhat "different." I don't use the term "different" in a disparaging manner, but many (if not most) of these boys seem to have some sort of disadvantage associated with them. It might consist of behavioral problems, speech impediments, emotional struggles, or even learning disabilities (frequently ADHD), but they generally have some sort of physical or emotional "issue" that sets them apart from their peers. Often these differences cause them to be isolated and more comfortable in female company, which tends to be more compassionate and accepting. They tend to have trouble fitting in with their peer group. Because of the lack of male role models, they have adapted to being around only women. This makes them uncomfortable around males. This propensity also makes them easier prey to fall in with any social group that does accept them, such as gangs of other fatherless boys or unhealthy male role models of all types.

These observations are purely anecdotal on my part, but various studies appear to support the emotional struggles boys have without a father. The trauma and stress of losing their father, possibly combined with having only female influences in their life, manifests itself through a variety of problems.

In a study described in the book *Destructive Trends in Mental Health: The Well-Intentioned Path to Harm*, by Rogers Wright and Nicholas Cummings, kids with ADHD were paired with male therapists due to the noted absence of father involvement in the children's lives. The kids were given behavioral treatment with the therapists, and special attention was paid to developing a positive attachment to the male figure. At the end of the treatment, only 11 percent of the boys and 2 percent of the girls had to remain on medication. The authors of this study suggested that social forces may be major contributors to ADHD. Among these social forces are "the absence of positive father role models; the presence of a revolving door for negative male role models brought into the home; poor parenting; the need for order in the classroom when teachers are severely curtailed in meting out discipline; and a declining appreciation in our culture of what constitutes normal boy behavior."[3]

I frequently receive emails from mothers or relatives of boys who struggle mightily because they lack positive male role models. These boys have any number of problems, but it's pretty obvious that all of their troubles begin and end with the loss of their father. From the path they are headed down, they do not appear to have any chance of successfully living a healthy life. We have found the best, perhaps only, way to break this destructive cycle is to educate the mother on healthy masculinity and then introduce a positive male role model in the boy's life. Without that intervention, the fatherless boys of today will sire the next generation of fatherless boys tomorrow.

Role Modeling

A boy needs a father to be a role model for life for him. It's not that he is perfect and never makes mistakes. I certainly made many mistakes as a father, husband, and man and continue to do so. But the effort is important. A son who sees his father try to be the best role model possible is inspired by the effort itself—especially if the father admits his mistakes and learns from them. Many a boy was inspired by his father's example of manliness under pressure. Likewise, many have been dismayed or even destroyed by their father's absence or abuse.

In lieu of a father, boys need a man in their lives. For fatherless boys, direct intervention by positive male role models can make a difference. Fathers are the best choice, but nearly any man will do in a pinch. God has given men the ability to heal wounded boys just by spending time with them, by caring about them, by investing themselves in them, by sharing their masculine "essence" with them. And usually a man doesn't even have to do anything special. Oftentimes it is just letting a boy stand next to him and watch what he does and how he does it that spreads spackle into the gap in his soul, healing the tear.

Many times when a boy from a divorced home reaches his teen years, he starts acting out. Mom can't control him anymore, so she sends him to live with his dad or to the farm to live with Grandpa. Boys instinctively seem to know they need that male influence in their lives. They may even subconsciously act out in order to force getting sent to live with their fathers or in another masculine environment.

In the movie *Gran Torino*, Clint Eastwood plays Walt Kowalski, a retired Korean War vet living in a changing neighborhood dominated by immigrants. Kowalski catches the fatherless Hmong teenage boy next door trying to steal his prized 1972 mint condition Gran Torino as a gang initiation. As penance the boy must work for him cleaning up the neighborhood. Kowalski develops a grudging respect for the boy and begins to teach him the way of manhood. He teaches him to work and how to fix things, to persevere through difficulties, how to talk like a man, and he models how a man protects those under his umbrella. He eventually gives his life to save the boy in a Christlike sacrifice. As the movie ends, a boy who was once hopeless has bloomed and now has a chance to succeed in life all because of the mentoring from an older man.

Theodore Roosevelt's father played a huge role in his life, even to the point of giving him health. Young Teddy called his father the "best man I ever knew." When Teddy was four, his father began spending long periods of time away from home working with President Lincoln during the Civil War. Biographer Edmund Morris describes what happened to young Roosevelt during his father's absence:

> The child was simultaneously sinking into what seemed like chronic invalidism. From the moment his father left home, the catalog of Teedie's [Teddy's] ailments became continuous. He suffered from coughs, colds, nausea, fevers, and a congenital form of nervous diarrhea. . . . On top of all this his asthma was worsening. . . . Lack of appetite brought about symptoms of malnutrition. . . . How much Teedie's asthma was aggravated by the absence of his father may be inferred from some remarks he made thirty-seven years later: "Handsome dandy that he was, the thought of him now and always has been a sense of comfort. I could breath [sic], I could sleep, when he had me in his arms. My father—he got me breath, he got me lungs, strength—life."[4]

But his father did not coddle him—in fact he pushed him quite strenuously. After being sickly his entire childhood, by age twelve young Roosevelt was tall, puny, frail, skeletal, and physically weak. His father told him, "Theodore, you have the mind but you have not the body, and without the help of the body the mind cannot go as far as it should. You must *make* your body. It is hard drudgery to make one's body, but I know you will do it."[5] Teddy immediately began a strenuous workout regimen that, through rigid self-discipline and determination, eventually built his body into one that became famous as being "as strong as a bull moose." His health improved and he went on to become an accomplished naturalist, writer, hunter, ranchman, conservationist, athlete, soldier, and politician who at forty-two years of age became the youngest president of the United States and one of the greatest men our country has ever produced.

We often take fatherless boys along with us camping as a group of men or on father-son activities. Some of these boys are quite tenderhearted and lovable but invariably very immature. They have been kept as Mommy's little boy. These boys spend too much time in the company of women and become uneasy or uncomfortable in the company of men. Because they spend so much time around female authority figures, they have developed feminized traits in their behavior. They do not understand the "rules" of masculine company. For instance, they talk too much, frequently interrupting men who are talking (which seems to be an acceptable communication technique among women but is considered disrespectful among men), and react emotionally inappropriately. They chatter incessantly without ever coming to a point in the conversation. These boys have not learned the unwritten "laws" of respect that men live by with one another. By interrupting the conversation with inappropriate anecdotes, they quickly alienate other males who can become scornful and contemptuous of them, eventually shunning and ignoring them.

They are also often disrespectful because they have been allowed to act that way around the women in their lives. It requires men to reprimand them—often harshly—to teach them how to behave appropriately in the company of men. Otherwise, men and other boys will not want to be around them, further isolating them, with devastating consequences as they get older. If they do not learn these skills and "toughen" out of their "softness," they suffer throughout their lives. They do not understand the more rough-hewn behavior of men, especially in the outdoors where men are more blunt in their behavior. They need to learn to ignore scrapes and bruises, not to fret over a cut, and to be enthusiastic in the face of adverse conditions or disappointments (there is nothing worse than a whiny, gloomy, complaining companion on a camping trip). Around their mothers these boys have learned that all they have to do is complain or act petulant and mom or grandmother will go to great lengths to fix their problems. To become healthy, happy men, these boys need to learn to fix their problems for themselves.

On a recent father-son camping trip, I took a nine-year-old fatherless boy as my helper. I spent most of the weekend using object lessons to teach him important life lessons. When he would interrupt a conversation, I would bring it to his attention and make him wait until the men talking were finished. When he would chatter incessantly, I would tell him to stop and be quiet for a while. I told him that men are frequently quiet as it allows us to think and process information. Talking is the way women process information—and that was what he had learned from the world of women he was surrounded by. When he would lose his pocketknife, I would make him search for it and miss activities until he found it as a lesson to be more responsible (twice I picked it up from the dirt and kept it in my pocket so it didn't get lost).

As we were packing up to leave, I made him take down his own tent and pack all his own gear. He struggled with many items. Each time he whined that he needed help, I would first encourage him to continue with tips, then ask him if he had tried everything possible, finally tell him to just keep at it. I also gently but firmly reminded him that men do not cry and whine during times of struggle, only girls do (I can hear the feminists howling already). Each time he insisted, "I can't!" I explained that the word "can't" is a form of a swear word. It might be the worst swear word in the English language, and please stop swearing at me. (To insist you "can't" do something is to deny God's power to work through us—something I'm sure God considers blasphemous.)

During one such episode he was near tears, and I finally patiently told him if he couldn't get it packed we would just leave his gear in the woods. He looked at me incredulously and said, "You mean you wouldn't help me with this?" I told him, "No, because if I do it for you, you'll never learn how to do it for yourself." See, he had been trained that if he just struggled and then became frustrated and whined enough, his mother would do it for him. He eventually persevered and finished all of the tasks by himself, learning a big lesson in self-competence. I praised him mightily, reminding him how he did not think he could do it, and yet he did. I told him that I must have had more faith in his ability than he did. He walked a little taller among the other men as we said good-bye to leave.

This boy's need for masculine affection was strong as well. This need manifested itself by walking a fine line, alternating between exhibiting the feminine overtures common among females (such as holding hands, touching faces, whispering endearments, and hugging) and his natural craving and desire for healthy masculine affection and touch—like punches, chest bumps, wrestling, banging fists, high fives, or a quick shoulder hug.

Fathers and Discipline

Fathers are especially important in disciplining children. Fathers have been endowed by God with the mantle of authority within the family. Children have an innate fear factor of fathers that they don't of their mothers. Edmund Morris describes it thus: "There hung about his big, relaxed body an ever-present threat of violence, like that of a lion who, dozing, will suddenly flick out a lethal paw."[6]

Especially for teen boys, fathers are the boundary that keeps them from asserting their will in ways that could be destructive to themselves and others. Fathers are routinely viewed as the enforcer of family rules and values. You seldom see gang members with involved, loving fathers at home. Teenage boys may even start to get mouthy with Mom at this stage in ways they would never try with their father.

Boys who are not disciplined by their fathers do not learn self-discipline, which is a huge factor in male satisfaction in life. Those who are undisciplined are unhappy and grow up to be men who disappoint others in their life.

Boys and young men also need to be tested as part of the maturation process. Those who never test themselves against life never find out what they are made of. They never become confident and secure in their manhood. Trials mature a man in ways that books or lectures never can. If boys are rescued (typically by female mentors) too often growing up, they never learn self-reliance and the skills to succeed in life. Most often a boy needs a man to help teach him to navigate his way through the brambles and thornbushes of manhood. Without that guidance, too many young boys and men grow up angry, frustrated, anxious, and scared. Too often they compensate for that by exhibiting a false sense of bravado and self-confidence. I remember as a young man being angry, defensive, and brash as a way to cover my insecurities. I was insecure because I never had a father figure guide me and teach me how to solve life's problems.

The truth is, if we continue to produce greater and greater numbers of angry young men, we will eventually experience an apocalyptic meltdown within our culture. When boys do not learn how to solve problems in life, they rely on others to take care of them instead of fulfilling their roles as protector and provider to the people they are responsible for. This failure then contributes even more to them feeling like a disappointment in life.

Without the modeled behavior from a father, a boy is left to try to navigate through life and all of the difficult circumstances that he will face. Boys without fathers are at a big disadvantage in every area of life. Many never recover and so spread destruction and pain wherever they go. Those who do recover struggle with issues their entire lives. Fatherhood wounds are deep, jagged tears in a boy's chest that leave scar tissue in their wake.

The good news is that millions of healthy men have been raised just by their mothers—famous men such as Olympian Michael Phelps and even great men such as General Robert E. Lee were raised by single moms. But having a mom understand what a boy needs in order to grow into authentic manhood is a big step in breaking the cycle of disadvantage that he often faces without a father in his life.

Questions for Reflection and Discussion

1. Why are older men important in the lives of young men?

2. Do you believe the author's assertion that God gave fathers tremendous power to influence lives? In what way did your father influence your life? How does that affect the way you view masculinity?

3. How are boys impacted by not having a father?

4. Why do boys need to be "pushed" by men? What happens when they are not?

5

HEALTHY MASCULINITY

The Marks of Manhood

It is from numberless diverse acts of courage and belief that
human history is shaped. Each time a man stands up for
an ideal, or acts to improve the lot of others, or strikes out
against injustice, he sends forth a tiny ripple of hope.

Robert F. Kennedy

ALL MALES YEARN for greatness. They desire to be inspired. They have a heart for significance, to live for something greater than themselves. Unfortunately, few are able to live the life they crave.

As a culture, we have done a poor job of inspiring our young men with a vision of greatness. Too often, by the time our young males are in their late teens, they have already begun to wallow in cynicism, narcissism, and moral morass. They have become jaded and lost that spark of idealism and passion that allows the less common man to accomplish great things and overcome terrible circumstances. They have lost (or have never been taught) the vision that inspires them to live a selfless version of life. The vision that compels them to use the masculine power God has endowed them with to lift others beyond what they would be without his presence in their lives.

There is nothing more inspiring than seeing a group of clear-eyed, passionate young men in pursuit of a noble cause. And there is nothing more discouraging than seeing a gang of dispirited, broken young men, eyes and hearts guarded, with no sense of direction or honor in their lives. These males live for their own self-gratification and often use their power to prey upon others instead of protecting and providing for them.

Moms and dads both help boys best by first teaching them to understand a vision of what healthy masculinity is all about. Boys need mentors—they cannot successfully jump the broad chasm between boyhood and manhood by themselves. But that requires us as adults and as a culture to try to determine what authentic masculinity looks like and what it means. Without a foundational concept and distinct parameters, it is very difficult to teach a young man, much less hold him accountable to, some nebulous standard that is unclearly defined.

Then we need to help him achieve the standards that show him he is becoming a man. Since what a female thinks and says to a male plays a huge part in how he feels about himself as a man, a mom can not only help a boy achieve manhood by her words but also lift the bar of masculinity to a higher standard. A mom who lifts masculinity to a higher standard through her speech and actions plants the seed that women have expectations of men that go beyond his immediate self-gratification. He will then believe that he has a greater purpose in life and will strive to fulfill that destiny.

What Does Healthy Masculinity Look Like?

> A man does what he must—in spite of personal consequences, in spite of obstacles and dangers and pressures—and that is the basis of all human morality.
>
> Winston Churchill

Far too many boys head off into manhood without any idea what their roles in life are or how to perform them. For boys without involved male role models in their lives, this can be especially devastating. It is crucial that we train them to be prepared for their roles as leaders and providers for their families. Boys who are not trained are blown around like leaves in the wind, never having substance in life. Boys need to understand what their roles as men, fathers, and husbands entail as well as how to fulfill those roles. The world is a frightening place, but boys who have training and knowledge approach those roles with confidence. Boys who don't get that training at home will find advice from someone or somewhere—usually from sources that are not healthy.

One of the more sacred responsibilities of a man is to protect his family from the hardness of life. Boys who are never taught that role (or who have had abandonment modeled for them) have a hard time understanding and adjusting to it. They fail to get the general satisfaction and feelings of manliness that come from fulfilling this role.

Important Attributes

Certain traits are fundamental core issues for males. Males primarily develop their self-esteem, self-image, and self-confidence through their accomplishments. Manhood often relies upon performance for its validation. Females, on the other hand, develop those traits through relationships with family, friends, and other people.

Michael Gurian describes it this way: "Boys need to compete and perform well to feel worthy. . . . A boy who is not being taught skills, shown how to compete successfully, and given praise for his success, feels lost."[1]

Males learn best by hands-on trial and error. They learn from their mistakes—by failing, getting back up, and retrying until they succeed. My stepfather never taught me how to fix a car when I was growing up. But by trying different things over and over again, I succeeded in fixing whatever the problem was. I taught myself enough about cars that I am now comfortable working on them. This same strategy has applied to almost everything I have ever done in life—including my relationships. The ability to teach myself through trial and error has contributed significantly to my self-esteem as a man. I know that I can do pretty much anything I set my mind to if I so choose. That means I am less likely (although not entirely immune) to feel threatened or defensive when challenges come along or I find myself in a situation that I have no experience in. Those feelings of competency are important to my identity as a man.

However, not having been taught to work with my hands and fix things by a father figure has been a source of frustration and anxiety my entire life. Having to teach myself means it takes three times as long with twice the mistakes! Nevertheless, the challenges I have overcome (whether it was coming from an abusive alcoholic family, starting several successful business enterprises from scratch, or staying married to one woman when divorce is my heritage) have developed a quiet self-confidence within me that keeps me going when other people might quit.

Boys who avoid life's challenges fail to develop self-esteem and self-confidence. Boys who quit or are rescued and not allowed to fail never develop the confidence and feelings of adequacy and competence so key to a male's self-esteem. When they do fail, they need to be encouraged to keep going, not criticized or enabled.

Women as Rescuers

> A woman simply is, but a man must become. Masculinity is risky and elusive. It is achieved by a revolt from woman, and it is confirmed only by other men. . . . Manhood coerced into sensitivity is no manhood at all.
>
> Camille Paglia

Females can destroy healthy masculinity even while trying to help it. Many moms, either through guilt or training, rush to keep their sons from experiencing any unpleasantness in life. This teaches boys to rely on women instead of learning to be self-sufficient and developing leadership skills.

Males who do not learn to be self-sufficient learn to take the easy way out of life's circumstances. Reliance upon a woman is an easy way out. Because of a mom's nurturing nature, she is wont to do everything she can to make sure her son is healthy, happy, safe, and content.

But a mom who does too much teaches a boy to depend upon a woman to meet all of his needs and desires.

One of the more shocking revelations the boys we take camping come to rather quickly is that the men are not there to serve them. The first time they plop down in a lawn chair around the campfire and expect a man to bring them something, they learn very quickly the folly of that attitude. They learn if they want something they need to get up and get it for themselves—and they might even lose their chair in the process! That brings up another good point. I've observed several situations where boys stayed in their chairs while Mom was willingly forced to stand. That does not go over well in our camps. If an adult (especially a woman) needs a chair, the boy gives up his—willingly or unwillingly. It is part of teaching a fundamental respect for elders that has been lost in our culture. It also teaches a respect for authority figures and for women. Besides, I am too old to stand while a youngster sits around idly pretending the world owes him something. Too many times Mom allows this to happen and her husband does not force the boy to give up his chair. In particular this level of respect needs to be given to Mom. Done properly throughout childhood and adolescence, it subtly instills a level of respect for all women in his life.

One thing that is important to remember is males (young or old) will generally always try to find the easy way to do something or get out of doing it. And so if a woman offers to do a task for them, they are more than willing to allow her. This is probably a survival skill developed over thousands of years where conserving your energy to hunt for food or defend yourself was a prerequisite for survival. Today, males do not have that excuse, however, and need to recognize their propensity to put things off or procrastinate until someone else does them. Continually serving a boy (or a man) creates that expectation. I believe it also eventually creates a certain level of disrespect for the woman. It is one thing to be nurturing or polite; it is another to be in a position of subservience or treated as a servant.

Steel and Velvet

> The world is a dangerous place to live; not because of the people who are evil, but because of the people who don't do anything about it.
>
> Albert Einstein

In his book *Man of Steel and Velvet*, Aubrey Andelin talks about the importance of men being both strong and tender. He likens a man's character to a building having a strong foundation of steel to support the structure, while the interior decorations, artwork, and landscaping are like velvet that smooths off the rough edges, adding beauty and softness.

Because boys are not being trained and mentored to high standards of masculinity, we are producing more and more men who are spoiled, spineless, and lacking in moral, physical, and mental strength. Unfortunately, when we produce men like this, it affects not only their lives but those around them as well and, in turn, negatively impacts all of society. Weak-kneed men eventually force women to become dominant mothers and take leadership roles they resent and are often frustrated with. When men do not fulfill their natural roles, this then prevents mothers from fulfilling their roles and responsibilities. Or as Andelin says, "If she must be the *man of the family*, she isn't free to function as a woman, to devote her time and thought to making a success of her equally demanding duties as a wife and mother."[2]

Additionally, the children of weak men suffer. They grow up feeling insecure due to lack of firmness and decisiveness. They never learn to respect or yield to authority. Growing up in a home where a father does not demand obedience, they learn only disobedience.[3] This creates all sorts of problems for their future families and society in general.

The following quote from Andelin describes the *strong* side of masculinity perfectly. Listen, though, to how politically incorrect this definition sounds today:

> A man of steel is a masculine man. He is aggressive, determined, decisive, and independent. He is efficient in a man's world, demanding quotas of himself in reaching his objectives. He is competent in a task, fearless and courageous in the face of difficulty, and master of a situation. He has convictions and steadfastly holds to these convictions. He sets high goals, goals which require dedication and patience. He is not afraid of strain and diligence. He rejects softness and timidity. When he has made a decision based on his best judgment, he is unbendable as a piece of steel. These qualities set him apart from women and weaker members of his own sex.[4]

The standard we have set today for masculinity is pitifully low. The changes that feminism brought to eliminate bad behaviors of masculinity also threw chivalrous and good behavior out like babies with the bathwater. Male role models of high standards are few and far between in today's cultural climate.

I am disgusted with corporate America for embracing gangsta rap stars as spokespersons and role models for their products. These are men whose music promotes violence and misogynistic attitudes toward women. Their personas and all they stand for and the values they promote are unhealthy for young men and women. To hold them up as healthy role models of manhood to our youth is unconscionable.

Boys and men who don't stand for anything, stand for nothing. Men who promote bad standards weaken the entire fabric of society, much like a crack in a concrete foundation. And males who are soft like velvet with no steel girding cannot be relied upon to use their masculine strength to give respite to those who are vulnerable, tired, or wounded and who look to them for protection and provision. Society at large suffers, due to their cowardly passivity and self-serving apathy.

What Does Authentic Masculinity Look Like?

The hottest place in Hell is reserved for those who remain neutral in times of great moral conflict.

Martin Luther King Jr.

Jamaican singer and musician Bob Marley believed that love and music could fight evil and darkness. In December 1976, two days before a free concert to ease tension between two warring political groups, Marley, his wife, and manager Don Taylor were wounded in an assault by unknown gunmen inside Marley's home. Taylor and Marley's wife sustained serious injuries but later made full recoveries. Bob Marley received minor wounds in the chest and arm. The shooting was thought to have been politically motivated, in an attempt to stop the concert. Nonetheless, the concert proceeded, and an injured Marley performed as scheduled, two days after the attack. When asked why,

Marley responded, "The people who are trying to make this world worse aren't taking a day off. How can I?"[5]

Marley understood that evil flourishes when good men stay silent or hide from adversity. It's a lesson that young men need to learn if they are to make the world a better place to live.

Even though I write and speak about authentic masculinity and have researched it extensively, I am not sure that I or anyone else can adequately describe it in just a few words. Entire volumes have been written about it. However, I think I can give you some general guidelines on what I think constitutes healthy, authentic masculinity and what doesn't.

Before we can produce good or great men, we must have an understanding of what healthy masculinity looks like. If boys and men are supposed to be masculine, then what exactly does masculinity mean? What does it mean to actually *be* a man? We tell boys and young men to act like a man, be a man, take it like a man; and yet we are not told *why* we need to "take it like a man" or "act like a man," much less *how* to be a man. Without someone to show us how a man faces life and solves problems, or at least a valid definition of manliness, we are left to figure out these and other mysteries of life on our own.

Some of the old models of masculinity we've had in the past don't seem to be quite as applicable today. For instance, the "big boys don't cry" mentality isn't accurate anymore, if it ever was. As a man, I have all the same emotions as every other human being. I might not be as in touch with or even able to identify them as readily as my wife, but I have feelings nonetheless. Just because I don't make a big deal out of them doesn't mean they don't exist. In addition, society has a very skewed perspective on what it means to be a man—mostly defined by wealth, power, toughness, sexual conquests, and the accumulation of material goods.

On the other end of the spectrum, the current cultural push to "feminize" males isn't very comfortable either. It's why so many boys and young men are confused. Society has spent the better part of the past several decades trying to soften or even feminize our young men and boys. Now we are confused and angry when they don't act more like real men. Males were created different from females for a reason. Now some people are looking to define a type of masculinity that combines the best of traditional manliness (strength, honor, character) with positive traits traditionally associated with females like nurturance, communicativeness, and cooperation. This might be an ideal goal for masculinity, but it may be more than the average guy can live up to.

Our culture generally tells us that, at best, the role of a man is to put his nose to the grindstone after finishing school and work hard the rest of his life. It tells us the mark of a man is how much money he makes and how many "toys" he acquires. His financial achievement determines how successful he has been in life. The American Dream is the standard by which we judge the success of a man's life. Cultural masculinity appears to hinge on the combination of power, the adoration of many females, sexual prowess, and the ability to make money (lots of it).

Because of that indoctrinated vision of masculinity, many men today are caught up in the self-centered, mundane pursuits of life. Most are apathetic and living lives filled with passivity—they lack decisiveness and commitment. They fail to see the higher purpose they were created for. Even the best of them often feel they are doing enough just by being a good guy, a caring person who does nice things for others occasionally—when it's convenient, that is.

If you watch nearly all of the recent movies created for young males, such as *Pineapple Express, Knocked Up,* and *Superbad,* the highest standard a young man can attain is to be "nice." All of the young male characters in these popular movies also just happen to be very self-centered and self-focused, wasting their masculine essence on self-gratifying pursuits like irresponsible sex, smoking pot, and surviving without working for a living. It is a popular "slacker" model of masculinity that is sweeping over our young men like a tidal wave. (By the way, I've watched all those movies and I think they are funny too . . . which makes their influence all the more dangerous for young men.)

Most men in our country today are trapped in societal expectations and the search for self-gratification. But I believe all men yearn for something meaningful, a cause to fight for—significance in our lives. What men fail to realize is that freedom lies in following God's plan for our lives. That plan requires us to be bold, take risks, and submit ourselves to the burdens and uncomfortable trials that God puts in our path to stretch and grow us.

Unfortunately, men who follow that path are often shunned by society or at best ignored. You seldom read in newspapers about men who make a difference in the world or see them interviewed on the evening news. In fact, our culture seems to consider an authentically masculine man to be dangerous. They would like to emasculate and prevent him from exerting his influence in the world. They use fear, shame, and political correctness to keep him silenced on the sidelines of life.

But men who attain authentic masculinity resist this attack and use their strength to make a difference in the world. An authentically masculine man puts aside his needs, desires, wants, and sometimes even his dreams, for the benefit of others. He does this without fanfare and frequently without anyone even noticing. His life is not about *his* individual rights, achievements, or happiness; it's about making life better for others. His sacrifices are part of his character and give his life significance. He meets these sacrifices with the stoic nobility that God granted all men by right of their birth gender.

Too many boys grow up thinking that manhood is finally having the freedom of not having to do things you don't want to do or of doing only what you want. I see fatherless boys who grow up thinking the world is about them and that women will serve and rescue them from every trouble and inconvenience they experience. But the reality is that being a man actually means being *required* to perform many things you don't want to do. It also means not doing many things you'd like to do.

A real man has honor. He stands tall as the fierce winds of adversity blow around him. He cherishes and protects women and children. He knows he has an obligation to mentor those who follow in his footsteps. He recognizes his sphere of influence and uses it for good. He understands that life does have fundamental truths and lives his life according to a firm set of principles. He uses his God-given warrior spirit to fight for justice and equality. He stands for *something*. Too many men today stand for nothing—they are directionless.

Men who exhibit authentic masculinity live lives of significance. They lift up others to help them achieve their potential. They make sacrifices in order to make a difference in the world—for everyone, not just their own family. They have passion and vision and are genuinely interested in giving of themselves for the betterment of others. And they probably don't make a big production out of doing it either. Men like this are other-centered, not self-centered. They are other-focused instead of self-focused.

I think it is imperative that we look to the Bible as a source of defining masculine behavior. Manhood as defined by the Bible requires men to put the needs and best interests of others before their own. It's about living sacrificially. A man uses his strength and influence to help others and defend those who cannot defend themselves.

Read how manly this passage from the book of Job, chapter 29, sounds and how it speaks powerfully to a man's heart:

> I rescued the poor who cried for help,
>   and the fatherless who had none to assist
>   him. . . .
> I made the widow's heart sing. . . .
> I was eyes to the blind
>   and feet to the lame.
> I was father to the needy;
>   I took up the case of the stranger.
> I broke the fangs of the wicked
>   and snatched the victims from their teeth.
>
> vv. 12–13, 15–17

God gives men a mandate throughout the Bible to protect women and children and be his representative here on earth. Authentic men are passionate, fierce, and noble—they care. In fact, they are dangerous, but it's a good dangerous.

Questions for Reflection and Discussion

1. Are young males today mired in "cynicism, narcissism, and moral morass"?

2. Why is it important for boys and young men to have a vision of what constitutes healthy masculinity?

3. What are some important attributes young men need to develop?

4. What happens when women rescue boys too much?

6

EMOTIONS

Developing a Healthy Emotional Life

The happiness and unhappiness of the rational, social animal depends not on what he feels but on what he does; just as his virtue and vice consist not in feeling but in doing.

Marcus Aurelius (121–180)

I LOVE WATCHING FOOTBALL. I used to love playing it when I was in high school. Football is an emotionally intensive game. Most coaches encourage players to play with a certain level of emotion because it amplifies a player's ability to perform. However, I have noticed a trend among many players today, even professionals. These players play at such a high emotional level that they cannot control themselves. Their uncontrolled emotional responses on the field often lead to dumb penalties and mental mistakes that hurt their teams. These players are unable to keep themselves from breaking the rules even when they know it will result in a penalty.

The truth is, men who cannot control their emotions hurt their families as well. I encourage young men to be passionate about life, to care about things. I want my son and my future son-in-law to be passionate about things that matter in life—social injustices like prejudice, discrimination, and racism; or crimes against humanity such as abuse, genocide, and human trafficking. Men who are passive and apathetic waste their gifts and never lift others up to greater heights. But I also want them to be able to appropriately control their emotions. I don't expect them to be robotic or even stoic, but I don't want them out of control and allowing their feelings to cause them to make snap judgments and decisions. I do not want them making decisions based solely on how they *feel* at any given time. Doing this causes men to say and do hurtful things to those they love when they are angry. It causes them to satisfy their lusts in inappropriate ways when they feel justified in demanding instant gratification. It causes them to be self-indulgent when they want an appetite satisfied or fulfilled. This emotional immaturity is destructive to them and the people around them.

Fear

Understanding a male's emotional life begins with recognizing the factors that cause him fear. Fear is one of the biggest motivators of a human being. Understanding what males are fundamentally afraid of can give us insight into their psyche and help us develop strategies to compensate for and overcome those issues.

Over the years many men have shared their fears with me. All males have certain fears that are strong within them regardless of age. These fears are probably similar in some ways to fears that women have, but I've observed that these fears are intensified in males.

The following are universal fears that most males (both boys and men) seem to share in common. They might not always be spoken of, but they linger within the hidden consciousness of a boy or a man.

One very honest man told me, "I have many fears that rule my life. I have a fear of failure and a fear of change or the unknown. It causes me to be excessively critical and pessimistic when faced with new challenges as a way to avoid them. It is debilitating and paralyzing when I allow this fear to dominate me."

Males have a great fear of being inadequate. Whether accurate or not, to feel and be perceived as inadequate is emasculating to males. To be incompetent is just as bad, since it means they lack the skills or ability to perform up to expectations. As they get older, this fear manifests itself in areas such as being afraid of not being able to perform sexually, being rejected by women, and not being able to provide financially and materially. Performance is important to males because this is how their self-esteem is developed. Males develop self-esteem through their accomplishments, while women typically develop theirs through relationships with others. This is why the folly of the recent strategy of "telling" boys how good they are (whether they had earned it through their accomplishments or not) was such a dismal failure in creating healthy male self-esteem.

Because to fail at something or appear inadequate is one of the greatest fears of a male, not understanding how to fulfill his responsibilities can cause a male to walk away or never even try if he thinks he will fail. I once spoke to a man from South Korea who told me they had a very high rate of fatherlessness. When I asked him why that was, he said, "Because our economy is struggling and there is a high unemployment rate. Men would rather abandon their families than face the humiliation of not being able to provide for them." I don't think that is a cultural phenomenon unique to South Korea.

All males have a fear of failure. To fail is to be branded inadequate or incompetent. While men fear failure, it's not the same as being inadequate. When we fail, we just get back up (hopefully), but being inadequate is humiliating. It means we cannot "cut the mustard" as a man. Men or boys who act overly macho—who push people around—are that way because they are afraid of being inadequate. They are weak, insecure, and scared. They try to compensate for that by making others afraid and, in that way, making others just like they are, which in turn makes them feel normal. Men raised without fathers often experience apprehension about becoming fathers or husbands themselves because they never had those roles modeled for them. They do not feel adequate to those huge and somewhat overwhelming roles. Additionally, they do not understand how a man is supposed to treat a woman (or love one) because that was never modeled for them either.

Males fear not being respected. Respect is a huge factor in a man's life. Often respect is more affirming to a male than love is. To be disrespected is emasculating and causes humiliation in a male. Humiliation then fuels feelings of inadequacy and incompetence in a never-ending cycle of ego destruction. One way to understand this need is to know that if a man's wife (or a boy's mother) does not respect him, then other males will not respect him either. This is because males have a hard shell they present to the world that covers their vulnerable underbelly of secretly feeling inadequate and unworthy. The woman in his life is often the only one who ever sees the inside of this shell, if only in glimpses. Mothers often set the tone of respect (and thus self-esteem) that a boy feels about himself and will expect from his wife.

Many males fear losing control. To not be in control is to be more likely to risk failing and thus to be vulnerable. This is one reason that emotions are so frightening to them. Emotions are powerful and often uncontrollable. Males with their lack of emotional competency and com-prehension (unlike females) are frightened by the power and wildness of emotions. In fact, most males consider emotions, or at least a strong show of emotions, to be a weakness. We are always slightly embarrassed by strong demonstrations of emotions, especially in other males.

Males also fear being dominated. It smacks of being in-adequate but also of being powerless to do anything about it. There are options to being inadequate, such as train-ing yourself or running away. When a man is dominated, there are not as many options. To be dominated is to be humiliated as a man. Men know that losing sometimes is inevitable, but being dominated is unbearable. It's one of the reasons pro football has rules against "taunting" an opponent.

Not being masculine enough is another big fear males have—not being masculine enough means not being con-sidered a man. Most guys would rather suffer through any physical pain than not be considered a man—that's why being disrespected by his wife (or mother) is so painful. When the one person (especially a woman) who knows him best treats him with disrespect, it is like saying to the world that he is not man enough.

Boys may also be what would be considered homophobic in our culture today. Even young boys have a fear of homosexuality as it causes them to question their masculinity. It is a threat to their unexplored and insecure manhood. Males who are secure in their manhood are seldom threatened by being too close to homosexuality.

For boys who struggle with developing or being comfortable with their masculinity, one area that we can encourage them in is observing, understanding, and nourishing the differences between males and females. Boys who learn to nourish their masculine bent toward work, fearlessness, determination, and even healthy aggressiveness develop an inner pride that God placed within their gender. This encourages them to strive to succeed when things are difficult. We can also encourage boys to recognize and consciously avoid more feminized traits such as hesitancy, indecisiveness, vacillation, softness, and other feminine mannerisms of speech and body movement. One illustration of this is that a young man in training should be able to garner all the facts of a specific circumstance, compare the pros and cons of the situation, project the outcomes, and make a firm decision within a relatively short period of time. A male who does not learn to make a decision is a constant source of frustration to those who depend upon him. While learning to do this, he may make mistakes—that's okay. He learns from his failures. Better to learn under your guidance than without that safety net.

Loss of significance is a big fear for males. The demotion or loss of a job, being ridiculed, or even having a baby or sibling take your place at home are demoralizing and frightening to males. Boys who lose their leadership status, fail to achieve a goal like making band or the chess club, or get cut from the team are demoralized.

Rejection is also very difficult for most males. It keeps us from attempting greatness. But even on a smaller scale the sting of rejection bites deep. Not getting the recognition we feel we deserve, being picked last to be on a team, even being ignored by a girl are subtle stabs to our manhood. And it only gets worse as we get older.

Males need to feel adequate and competent in order to feel good about themselves. A mother can use her feminine influence (which is huge) to help her son properly develop the following characteristics that will prevent him from having the fears that hold men back in life.

Anger

Anger produces a physiological arousal in males. It creates a state of readiness and heightened awareness. It creates energy that can be directed outward in the form of protection or even as a weapon. Anger causes a fight-or-flight response designed to protect us. Anger is frequently a powerful tool boys and men use to cover our inadequacies. Oftentimes anger in males is a secondary emotion used to cover underlying emotions such as fear, hurt, or frustration. You'll notice that young and even older males will react with anger when they become overly frustrated or are hurt emotionally.

The surge of adrenaline and associated arousal can be addicting to some males. Young males need to be taught how to deal with and control their anger. In order to do that, they must learn to own their anger and identify the source of that anger. Then they can learn to determine how to choose to respond to their anger.

Males are not very adept at understanding their emotions nor very comfortable dealing with them. Emotions are powerful and often uncontrollable. That's why many males keep such a tight lid on their emotions—once released they are difficult to predict or control and often result in a situation ending in vulnerability. The one emotion, however, that they are relatively comfortable with is that of anger. Anger for many men is an old friend, one they call upon in a variety of circumstances. Like all powerful emotions, it can be used destructively or for good. For instance, anger can be terribly destructive in relationships. After all, anger is only one letter away from being danger. All we need to do is look at the devastation caused to women and children through a man's uncontrolled wrath and anger. Anger can lead to emotional, psychological, and even physical abuse.

On the other hand, anger can be channeled into productive pathways. Anger can be used to motivate a man to achieve more than he might otherwise be able to accomplish. It can be used as a mechanism to encourage perseverance under duress or in grueling circumstances. Many a boy accomplished some difficult task all because he got angry when someone told him he couldn't succeed. When teased, many boys use that anger to motivate themselves to "prove" their offenders wrong. One method in coaching is to get young men angry in order to motivate them to perform beyond their self-imposed limitations. In fact, many men—myself included—propel themselves with anger and grit to succeed in life because a father figure constantly told them they wouldn't amount to anything. Warriors often used anger toward their enemies as motivation to succeed in battle or even in a school-yard fight.

Regardless of how it is used, anger is the emotion most familiar to males. Anger is often a secondary emotion used by males to cover or mask other emotions. For instance, certain emotions such as fear, anxiety, vulnerability, or distress often produce a feeling of humiliation in males. Humiliation is considered a weakness by males. Remember, for most males to show weakness is to be vulnerable and open to criticism. To be vulnerable is an invitation to be attacked. But anger is a defense against attack and may even be a weapon to attack others. Very angry men and boys are seldom messed with, even by bullies.

Rather than feel humiliated by these "unmanly" emotions, many males instinctively and automatically use anger to cover those feelings. Even pain (physical or psychological) can be covered by anger. Notice how most males react when they hit their thumb with a hammer. They'd rather get mad than cry. Most men also get angry rather than depressed or hysterical when faced with an emotional crisis in a relationship. Again, this is a protective mechanism for their fragile egos—egos that are covering secretly ingrained feelings of inadequacy and incompetence.

Sometimes anger is even used consciously. I was raised in an alcoholic and abusive home. I can distinctly remember at about the age of twelve when I first discovered that, if I just got angry, I didn't have to feel that humiliating emotion of being afraid. In typical naive boyhood fashion, I told myself, "This is great. I'll never be scared again for the rest of my life!" However, this was foolish, as I spent a significant portion of my adult life being angry. Angry because I was actually afraid—afraid because I had never had a positive male role model show me how a man lives his life and faces his problems in a healthy manner.

Young men who are not taught how a man acts, what his roles in life are, and how to fulfill them adequately and competently are very often angry. They are angry at life and at the world. They take this anger out on others, hoping to hurt them before they themselves are hurt, even if that hurt is just humiliation from their own ineptness.

Love

Love consists of joy and trusting another. For a male, to trust another person is to be vulnerable. Love and intimacy require a male to willingly allow himself to be vulnerable, which is against his nature. While boys grow up naturally learning to love their mothers, it is an emotion that males need to understand and see modeled in order to transfer it to another human being. Since visual observation is the primary way most males learn, this is also the best way for men to teach boys about love.

Parents provide a huge role model for boys on love and relationships. Young men who come from homes where a healthy marriage existed often talk about how helpful that was to them as a model and source of strength as they discover their place in the world and settle upon a belief/value system. For those who come from a broken home, however, the wounds incurred during their parents' divorce are more often identified than any benefits gained from a divorce.

Fathers model how a man is supposed to love a woman. Mothers model how a woman responds to a man's love. Loving a woman does not come naturally to most males. Watch the difference in how a young man who grew up with no healthy male role models treats his wife (or more often live-in lover) versus one who grew up with a father who loved the boy's mother.

For instance, a young man who grew up with healthy male role models has learned what it means to sacrifice for his family, while a man without that modeling will likely be naturally focused on his own needs and wants. Boys with positive male role models learn the intentionality of love—that love is a decision more than an emotion. They learn that the *actions* of loving a woman produce that feeling within them. They learn that love stays for the long haul and doesn't quit when things are difficult. And they learn that a long-term loving relationship has cycles of ups and downs that are a normal part of the relationship. Boys who don't learn that, or have that lesson short-circuited, end up failing to learn the sacrificial nature of love and the rewards that brings.

To give oneself sacrificially on a daily basis for the sake of another is not a natural male trait (although men willingly give their lives for others in war). In general, the opposite might even be true. I know women look hard to find and hang on to admirable traits in all their men, especially their sons, but to find males who are naturally loving, kind, gentle, and compassionate is unusual—at least in males who have not been feminized.

Loving a woman is a modeled behavior for a male. Learning to lead his family in a healthy manner is another modeled behavior that boys seldom learn from any other source. The respect that a father gives a boy's mother is the level of respect that he will think all women deserve. Appreciating the value that a woman brings to a relationship and the family is another gift that a father or other male role model gives to a boy. Learning to cherish and love a woman in the ways that she needs and not the ways that he feels more comfortable with is a lesson that a boy cannot get from any other source than from watching his father every day. Recognizing her more tender heart and the devastation that his words can have on a woman are taught to a boy by his father. And perhaps the greatest lesson a father passes along is the ability to admit he is wrong, to apologize, and to ask for forgiveness—not an easy thing for most males.

Lastly, love is an emotion we need more of in our world. We especially need men who are healthy enough to love others unashamedly and unabashedly. When males are able to do that, not only are their lives better but the world is a better place as well. Maybe our boys learn to be loving by being loved—loved by a mother *and* a father, grandparents, siblings, relatives, and friends. These many types of loves (for example, a loving relationship between a mother and son is different than a loving relationship between a grandfather and grandson) teach a boy to observe love from its many different perspectives and angles, giving him a well-rounded ability to love wholeheartedly instead of guarding his heart against possible pain and rejection. Our challenge is to figure out how to give our son the love he needs to grow up to be a man who is secure enough *to* love.

Aggression

Most males are comfortable with or at least knowledgeable of aggression in one form or another. Aggression generally has an element of anger in it. In our look at testosterone and its effects on the male body and psyche, we learned how that hormone contributes to male aggression. Likewise we noted earlier how wounded and insecure boys are frequently aggressive as a defense mechanism.

Like all emotions, aggression can be good or bad. Too much aggression is dangerous and volatile. Too little aggression creates passive, apathetic milquetoasts of men. Repressed aggression turns into passive-aggressive behavior that is destructive to the male and to his family and acquaintances. Uncontrolled aggression kills people and destroys civilizations.

Most males are probably created to be at least somewhat more aggressive than females. We see it in boys and young men who joyfully take dangerous risks with the potential for physical harm. We see it in men willing to take financial and career risks in order to further themselves. Aggression is part of the defense/protective mechanism built into the male role.

Our challenge is to raise boys into men who are balanced between too much and too little aggression. Healthy aggression prompts men to be leaders spiritually and with their families and communities. It provides and protects those who cannot fend for themselves.

Questions for Reflection and Discussion

1. Which emotions are males most familiar with? Why?

2. Why are many males angry?

3. Have you ever noticed your son using anger as a "secondary" emotion to cover other emotions such as fear, pain, vulnerability, or anxiety?

4. Why is it important to teach boys how to love?

7

DANGERS

There Be Dragons

*I looked, and there before me was a pale horse! Its rider
was named Death, and Hades was following close behind
him.*

Revelation 6:8

WHEN MAPMAKERS IN the olden days got to a point
where the land had not been explored yet, they
simply wrote: *Beyond this point there be dragons!* That
signified that there was potential danger ahead in the
unknown territory. Raising teenage boys can feel like we
are traveling through uncharted waters or an unexplored
wilderness. It can seem as though dangers are lurking
like wild beasts just waiting to leap out and ravage our

sons. The truth is, there are many dangers that our boys can unwittingly stumble into, sucking them under like quicksand. The following are some "dragons" you and your son need to watch out for.

Dangerous Times

Adolescence is a dangerous time for boys. Michael Gurian says, "Our culture has declared war on men and boys. The culture as we know it is harsh on young men, looks down on them, overreacts to them in fear, overreacts to masculinity in general, or neglects any particulars in masculinity that seem to take some hard work. All in all, we don't live in a very male-friendly time."[1]

Psychologists, such as William Pollock in his popular book *Real Boys: Rescuing Our Sons from the Myths of Boyhood,* insinuate that the majority of our sons are broken and that we are raising a nation of dysfunctional, unhappy boys. As Pollock says, "Boys today are in serious trouble, including many who seem 'normal' and to be doing just fine. Confused by society's mixed messages about what's expected of them as boys, and later as men, many feel a sadness and disconnection they cannot even name. New research shows that boys are faring less well in school than they did in the past and in comparison to girls, that many boys have remarkably fragile self-esteem, and that the rates of both depression and suicide in boys is frighteningly on the rise. Many of our sons are currently in a desperate crisis."[2]

Beyond just psychological discomfort, our boys are in physical danger as well. About 40 percent of teens surveyed said they knew someone in their age group who had been shot in the last five years. Approximately 20 percent of

125

all violent crime is committed by children under the age of eighteen.[3]

Boys (especially those with no training or mentoring) are more susceptible to a number of disadvantages and health threats in life, partially because they are hormone-driven and wired for aggression. Compared to girls, boys

- are four to five times more likely to be diagnosed with Attention Deficit Hyperactivity Disorder (ADHD)[4]
- commit 95 percent of juvenile homicides[5]
- are four times more likely to commit suicide[6]
- are six times more likely to have learning disorders
- are three times more likely to be drug addicts
- have a 50 percent greater risk of dying in a car accident
- comprise 90 percent of those in drug treatment programs and 95 percent of those involved in juvenile court[7]

Bullying in schools is also becoming an increasingly bigger problem. The American Psychological Association estimates that a shocking 90 percent of fourth through eighth graders report being victims of some form of bullying. Kids are subject to several forms of bullying, including physical, verbal, or social. Bullying is not just physical abuse limited to punching, pushing, or hitting. The internet and social networks provide unrestrained opportunities for bullies to abuse their victims with no accountability. This cyber-bullying, like spreading rumors and lies about another through spoken or written words via electronic media, is perhaps more destructive than physical abuse. Kids fear that everyone at school will see them bullied all over cyberspace—for example, on MySpace, Facebook, or Xanga, or through instant messaging, text messaging, email, blogs, cell phones, or chat rooms. The newspapers have been full of incidents where teens have been bullied to the point they have committed suicide (known as *bullycide*) in order to escape the abuse of both their peers and even adults.[8]

Paul Coughlin, author of *No More Christian Nice Guy*, writes, "One national poll revealed that at least a third of teens have had mean, threatening, or embarrassing statements made about them online. In Illinois alone, researchers estimate that a half million kids have been victimized by cyber-bullying. Ten percent were threatened with physical harm (which is a crime). There's even software that allows people to text and instant message people as if they are someone else. There is no conventional way of tracking down the impostor. The anonymity allows bullies to be even more malicious."[9]

Bullying of young men is also partially responsible for many of the school shootings the past decade. Teenage boys with poor self-esteem, an unloving home environment, and bad influences from peers and the media are bullied mercilessly until they finally snap in anger and frustration.

What complicates all this even further is that many young men today are immature, unfocused, and undirected longer in life. Part of the problem may be because many boys are being raised with lowered expectations. Plus our young people are raised with an entitlement attitude, expecting that the world owes them an easy life. One of the consequences of this is evidenced by the recent phenomena of the "failure to launch" syndrome, which is where young men continue to live at home with their parent(s) until their late twenties or even thirties.

Another factor might be that more males are being raised exclusively in the world of women, complicating their lives on many levels. One poor teenage boy at our Single Mom's Family Camp was being raised in a home with his sisters, his mother, his grandmother, and his great-grandmother. He was the only male presence in the entire house—even the dog was female. When he walked into his cabin, he said to his mother, "Look, we have a house all to ourselves!" His relief at being away from so much femininity was obvious. Single moms especially tend to surround themselves with other single moms who can understand their plight. Boys like this are faced with schools that are staffed almost exclusively with female teachers, female Sunday school teachers, female Cub Scout den mothers, and even female coaches. Their challenge is to try to understand a masculine perspective of life when all they see modeled is a feminine view of the world and a feminine response to life. Not that there's anything wrong with femininity—in reality, it is good; it's the way God created females. But like anything, too much of a good thing is bad for anyone, especially when there are no masculine role models (or only poor ones) to help offset the imbalance. We witness a plethora of young men today who expect women to take care of them and "rescue" them every time they get into trouble.

I know it has always been popular for the previous generation to think that the current crop of young people is out of control, but it truly appears that the current young generation of our culture has slid further faster than any previous generation. And it has all happened on our watch. The lack of male leadership in my generation allowed, enabled, and even encouraged the decline of values within our culture. Political correctness (or "re-education") has also caused many changes in our culture to take place, especially regarding young people. For instance, a lack of personal responsibility has been encouraged, the expectation of immediate gratification is the norm, disrespect for authority is encouraged, lack of personal integrity and honesty is now commonplace, and lack of respect and loyalty to our country has become acceptable and even fashionable. It seems as though common sense and hard work have been replaced by an entitlement mentality.

A young man will struggle to succeed with that kind of mind-set. Here are some of the other challenges that boys are faced with today.

The War on Boys

There has been both an overt and a more subtle, underlying attack on boys and masculinity over the past three or four decades. Ardent feminists have suggested that boys suffer from "testosterone poisoning" and that all normal male behavior is subjugating and abusive to women. As John Eldredge, author of *Wild at Heart*, says, "The idea, widely held in our culture, is that the aggressive nature of boys is inherently bad, and we have to make them into something more like girls."[10]

Popular psychologists, such as Mary Pipher in her book *Reviving Ophelia*, seem to suggest that whatever disadvantages girls may have in life are somehow the fault of boys. Her book has heavily influenced a generation of educators and government policy makers.

Christina Hoff Sommers, resident scholar at the American Enterprise Institute, well known for her critique of modern-day feminism, says, "It's a bad time to be a boy in America. As the new millennium begins, the triumphant victory of our women's soccer team has come to symbolize the spirit of American girls. The defining event for boys is the shooting at Columbine High."[11] She goes on to say that the media and feminists have portrayed boys to be the bane of society and the cause of most of its ills. The premise then, put forth by many special interest groups, is that we must eradicate natural masculine behavior in young boys through social engineering programs in the public schools and other venues.

Boys and young men in our culture are viewed with skepticism at best and fear at worst. Because young males are misunderstood, they are not nurtured in ways that help develop their self-esteem properly, causing them to either withdraw or lash out in frustration.

Our culture has declared war on masculinity in a variety of ways. For instance, nearly all television programs, commercials, and movies portray men in a bad light today. Men are typically portrayed as either abusive jerks or bumbling, incompetent idiots. This is most often presented under the guise of humor, which makes it psychically and socially palatable. Some of this criticism may be deserved, yet my concern is for the multitude of boys and girls who are being raised without a positive male role model in their lives to offset this stereotype. Since the media is one of the biggest influences of children, how will these young people envision men, husbands, and fathers and what their roles should be? How will boys feel about themselves, and what type of men will girls be drawn to?

Because of changes in our culture, a man's role has evolved over the years, and men are now confused as to what society expects of them. Frankly, the feminist movement, while bringing about some much-needed changes, also served to squash traditional male roles without providing a model to replace them. They have directly or indirectly demonized much of authentic masculine behavior to a generation of young people. Males have been taught that it was inappropriate, if not downright insulting, to honor and cherish women. That mentality has backfired on women today.

Males receive conflicting messages—some subconscious and some overt—from the media, churches, the political left and right, the government, and even our educational system. We've already produced a generation filled with men who have not had a role model of positive manhood in their lives. What happens when *their* children grow up without that role model as well?

Cultural Influences

One of the greatest challenges we face as a culture (and as parents) is defining healthy masculinity to a generation of young men and then inspiring them to achieve that vision. Unfortunately, our culture does not join us in desiring to promote a noble vision of manhood to boys.

Teens today face challenges you and I never dreamed of. They are bombarded daily by advertisers and media outlets that couldn't care less about what's healthy for children and only care about making money. Our kids today are desperate for the truth. They want to know what is right and what is wrong. They desperately want someone to show them that life can be good and healthy and fun, that marriages can last a lifetime, and that true love does indeed exist. They want (and need) to know that good and evil exist and are not just whatever a person believes to be true or not.

Yes, they are jaded and cynical sometimes, but they crave discipline and nurturing. They grew up exposed to video games that teach them how to plan a murder and carry it out, how to pick up a prostitute, how to steal cars and shoot guns. They watch endless television shows that teach them promiscuous sex is the road to happiness. Their innocence has been stolen by the greed of an uncaring and debauched culture. Boys are especially at risk in this world of decadence and sexualized glamour. Our young men are the future of our country, and yet too many are being ensnared in traps that sap their masculine energies from them.

The truth is, millions of young men in our country are falling through the cracks. They are failing in school, dropping out of church, becoming addicted to pornography or drugs, and leaving the families they create in droves. If we are to raise up men who will be leaders of families and communities and protectors of truth and justice, then we must first teach boys what it means to be a man—a real man. For far too long now our culture has lowered the bar on manhood. We have taught them that men are not valuable by criticizing and making fun of them at every turn. We have taught them that women are useful for irresponsible sexual gratification. We have taught them that fathers and husbands are not important.

Instead we need to teach boys their unique roles and responsibilities that God has given them. We need to help them embrace the gift of masculinity rather than consider it a liability. We need to encourage them in the areas in which they struggle and nurture them in those where they are proficient.

Teenage boys are especially susceptible to the unhealthy influences being perpetrated upon them by a culture seemingly bent on their destruction. For instance, video games are attractive to males because of the action, competitiveness, and hand-eye coordination required, but these same video games frequently contribute to their demise. They lead to lack of physical exercise, they desensitize boys to violence, and they create a shortened attention span that needs constantly greater amounts of stimulation in order to focus.

Unhealthy Influences

During adolescence, *peers* become increasingly important in the lives of teenagers. Friends provide a huge influence on how teens think, act, feel, and behave. Sometimes that is good and sometimes it is not. Many young people from good families have been led down the path of destruction, all because of the negative influence of unhealthy friends in their lives.

The entire time we raised our children, we had a sign on our family computer that read "Show me your friends and I'll show you your future." That didn't seem to make much difference in the kinds of kids our children chose to hang around with, but the sentiment is very accurate.

As a parent—even of older teens—it is our responsibility to protect our children from unhealthy influences. Many parents think this is a violation of their children's "rights" for an adult to interfere with their friendships. But we wouldn't hesitate to take action if our kids were hanging around with adults who were convicted pedophiles or known drug dealers. There's not much difference between those types of influences and the control that damaged or broken young people can have on our children's lives.

As a teen, our daughter always had a "rescuer" mentality. She generally picked the at-risk kids who didn't have a mother or a father and tried to be a good influence in their lives. While her compassion and intent were admirable, it often placed her in situations and circumstances that, had she had less-involved parents, would have resulted in disaster.

Certain unhealthy elements of our culture have your teen son in their sights as well. Behavioral scientist Dr. Randall Eaton says, "Popular music today features screams of agony, hate, desperation, self-pity, anarchy, loneliness, and suicide."[12] Movies and television shows promote irresponsible sexual promiscuity with no consequences. Role models such as professional athletes, musicians, and actors engage in criminal acts and irresponsible behaviors. Advertisers go to great lengths to instill a materialistic and narcissistic mentality in our youth. Pornographers target young men as lifelong consumers. And drug dealers, the sex trades, and the gambling industry are all interested in making money off the weaknesses of young males.

Education

A child miseducated is a child lost.

John F. Kennedy

The struggles boys are faced with in our society today are monumental. Young males face a crisis situation in our culture. Educationally, boys are failing at an alarming rate. Boys' reading and writing scores in school are abysmal. Boys have a much higher dropout rate than girls. Only 64 percent (just 50 percent of African Americans) of our boys now graduate from high school.[13] Fewer and fewer young men are attending college. In 2001, college enrollments consisted of 44 percent male and 56 percent female students.[14] According to the US Department of

Education, this trend of greater female than male college enrollment will continue, with the gap widening another 6 percent by 2013.[15] This means that in a few years, only about three out of ten college students will be male. Graduate degree rates are even more skewed in favor of females.

Michael Gurian describes the plight of teen boys in school today:

> Adolescent boys are twice as likely as girls to be diagnosed as learning disabled. Two-thirds of high school special education students are male. Adolescent males are four times more likely to drop out of high school than adolescent females. Adolescent males are much more likely to be left back a grade. And adolescent males on average get worse grades than females. The majority of salutatorians and valedictorians now are female. . . . Adolescent males are outscored by adolescent females by twelve points in reading and seventeen points in writing. The U.S. Department of Education recently pointed out that this gender gap in reading/writing is equivalent to about one and one-half years of school![16]

Michael Thompson, PhD, coauthor of *Raising Cain*, says, "But for the average boy, school is not as good a fit as it is for the average girl. More boys have problems with attention and focus than girls. Because of their higher activity level, boys are likely to get into more trouble than girls. And they are not given enough opportunities to move around—both in actual physical activity and in how they learn—because they spend too much time sitting and not enough time learning by doing, making and building things."[17]

The difference between reading and writing skills between teenage boys and their female counterparts is alarming. Every year I help review our local high school senior report projects. The writing skills of the girls far exceed the proficiency (like night and day) of the boys in nearly every case.

Because of the challenges boys face in schools, they often elect to drop out instead of stay. This is one way a male's frustration with this scenario is played out. Our current system of public education is clearly geared more toward the female style of learning—requiring sitting quietly for long periods while being lectured to, substantial amounts of reading and language comprehension (which males are typically poor at), verbal interaction by answering questions, collaborative learning, and writing essay-style reports. This causes boys, with their inability to sit quietly and listen to lectures for long periods of time, their difficulty with verbally expressing themselves, their lower reading and writing skills and longer cognitive processing time, to quickly fall behind girls in school. Boys learn to read later than girls do and often never become as proficient as females.

It doesn't take long for little Johnny to shut down and quit trying if he consistently gets beaten by a girl every time he tries to compete at educational activities. To succeed at schoolwork then quickly becomes a "feminine" trait because girls are good at school and boys aren't (except those with feminine strengths like verbal acumen). No boy wants to be like a girl. Since it is humiliating to fail (by being asked to read aloud when you can't read or answer questions verbally before you have had time to process them), especially in front of an entire class, males quickly quit trying. Because it is unmanly to be sensitive or to "act like a girl," little Johnny doesn't cry or complain about this, he gets angry and shuts down. He stuffs down his anger at the inequality and injustice of it all and becomes even more aggressive and potentially violent.

Most males appear to be uninterested and uninspired with school. But boys don't have a problem with education per se. Put them in a challenging, competitive, stimulating environment that teaches to their skill sets and watch how excited and passionate they become about learning. We see it in sports, outdoor activities, and even in the arts when teachers who understand boys employ male-friendly learning styles. Males in these environments flourish even when learning classical education subjects (see the movies *Dead Poet's Society* or *The Emperor's Club*).

I teach in completely different styles when I give workshops to men than I do when giving seminars to women. I use object lessons and visual aids with men. I give men more frequent breaks and allow them to move around the room at will. I use more video clips and less lecturing with males. I also use inspiring stories of action, adventure, and life-or-death situations. Lastly, I do not allow women in the room during a workshop as it changes the entire dynamics of the room when a woman is present. Males are less willing to be open and vulnerable with a woman present and will maintain a façade in her presence. Additionally, a woman is a constant distraction to a male's ability to concentrate.

If your son is struggling in school, I encourage you to find ways to help him succeed. Try to find passionate male teachers, although they are rare in a feminized public education environment that encourages passivity and softness in male students, teachers, and administrators. Get him tutoring to help in areas he struggles. Find programs that educate by using object lessons, solitary and reflective learning strategies, and all-male environments.

Additionally, consider the subject matter. Boys like topics with action, adventure, wars, and heroes. Most boys will even embrace poetry, music, classical literature, and reading if presented in the right format. Boys also seem to succeed in gender-specific environments. Students in all-boy schools and classrooms have much better test scores and educational outcomes than their peers in coed environments. In one of many schools experimenting with single-sex classrooms across the country, 57 percent of girls and 37 percent of boys passed a state writing test in the coed classrooms. In the single-sex classes, 75 percent of girls and 86 percent of boys passed.[18]

Also, encourage him to read. Even comic books or sports statistics provide opportunities to read. Hopefully, a male he looks up to enjoys reading. Leaders truly are readers.

The potential consequences of continuing to allow our boys to fail in the educational system and producing more and more angry, hopeless, frustrated young men are frightening at best and devastating at worst.

Drugs and Alcohol

Drugs and alcohol abuse continue to be two of the greatest threats that teenagers and young adults face today. By age fourteen, 35 percent of youth have engaged in some form of illicit (illegal) drug use. By the end of high school, more than 50 percent will have tried at least one illicit drug. Teens who begin using illicit drugs before the age of fifteen are more likely to develop a lifelong dependence on illegal substances.[19]

Besides the traditional drugs of choice like marijuana, hashish, cocaine, ecstasy, heroin, and alcohol, kids are also abusing other substances. Ingesting large amounts of

Adolescent Drug Usage

- **Marijuana** is the most prevalent illicit drug used by teens because it is easily accessible. In fact, 90% of high school seniors stated that obtaining marijuana is virtually trouble-free, and nearly 40% of 10th and 12th graders reported smoking marijuana. Teens who use this drug are more likely to initiate the use of other drugs (e.g., cocaine and heroin).
- **Ecstasy** is also a prevalent drug that is highly accessible and used at teen parties. Over the past few years, ecstasy use by teens has increased: one in thirty 8th graders and one in twelve 12th graders reported using ecstasy in 2000.
- **Heroin** is primarily injected into the vein but can also be inhaled nasally and smoked. While 8th graders' overall use of the drug is declining, 12th graders' use by means of inhaling is increasing.
- **Cocaine** has been a serious drug problem in America for almost a century. According to the National Institute on Drug Abuse (2001), 5% of 12th graders reported using cocaine in 2000.[20]

cough syrup containing dextromethorphan (DXM) causes visual hallucinations and a heightened awareness. Huffing is the use of inhalants such as spray paint (typically silver or gold), glue, shoe polish, gasoline or lighter fluid, or other solvents, degreasers, or cleaners. In 2000, over two million kids between the ages of twelve and seventeen reported using inhalants at least once. Pharm Parties are also gaining popularity. This is where a group of students comes together after having raided their parents' medicine cabinets and throws all the medications into a bowl. Participants then take handfuls of the medicines and wait to see the results.[21]

Methamphetamine (also known as meth, ice, crystal, crank, glass, or speed) is a highly addictive drug made from readily obtainable household chemicals. It triggers a release of dopamine and norepinephrine in the brain inducing intense euphoria. Among other symptoms, it causes the user to feel paranoia, anxiety, aggression, and feelings of power and superiority. Serious health and appearance problems are associated with meth use, including "meth mouth" (where teeth rot away) and abscesses on the skin. Meth addictions are one of the most difficult addictions to treat. Criminal behavior is often an associated outcome of meth use.[22]

Kids from single-parent homes are especially susceptible to drug and alcohol abuse. The Substance Abuse and Mental Health Services Administration stated in its report *The Relationship between Family Structure and Adolescent Substance Use* that no matter the gender, age, family income, or race/ethnicity, adolescents not living with both parents are 50 to 150 percent more likely to use substances, be dependent upon substances, or to need drug abuse treatment than adolescents living with two biological or adoptive parents.[23] Children growing up in single-parent households are at a significantly increased risk for drug abuse as teenagers.[24] Governmental surveys have shown that fatherless children are at a dramatically greater risk of drug and alcohol abuse, mental illness, suicide, poor educational performance, teen pregnancy, and criminality.[25]

Children from father-only families appear to fare as poorly or even worse. Using a sample of 22,237 adolescents ages twelve to seventeen from three years of data from the National Survey on Drug Abuse, it was found that even after controls were factored in, teens from mother-stepfather and mother-only homes were 1.5 to 2 times at risk for illegal drug use, and teens in father-only and father-stepmother families evidenced over 2.5 times the risk of illegal drug use compared to teens in mother-father families.[26]

Crime

I frequently speak to men in prisons across the country. I have spoken in medium security prisons and maximum security penitentiaries. I have spoken at prisons ranging from the Oregon State Penitentiary to Wildwood Correctional Facility in Kenai and Cold Spring Creek in Seward, Alaska, the most dangerous prison in the state. I recently spoke at a prison in St. Croix, US Virgin Islands, to incarcerated fathers and sons.

All of the men I speak to in prisons have one thing in common—they did not intend to end up there. The vast majority of them had no father or any healthy male role model in their life. Most of them can look back on their lives and point to the fact that they had a lack of discipline and appropriate boundaries in their home lives. Many were abused or neglected as children. They lack education and spiritual training. The education level of prison inmates is well below average compared to the normal population. Fully 60 percent of prison inmates are functionally illiterate.[27]

Most of the national prison population consists of young men. The average age of offenders in this country is eighteen to thirty-five, with young males outnumbering females ten to one. Violent offenses increased 82 percent between 1972 and 2000. In 2001 nearly 600,000 young men under the age of twenty-five were under some sort of correctional supervision.[28]

According to the US Department of Justice, in 2003 a total of over 2 million children under eighteen years of age were arrested for crimes committed, with over 92,000 of them being considered violent in nature. Another 4 million arrests were made of mostly young men ages eighteen to twenty-four for crimes committed.[29]

Being raised without a father or father figure greatly increases the risks for boys ending up in prison or committing a crime. Boys who grow up outside intact families are twice as likely to end up in jail. Every year spent living without a father increases the odds of future incarceration by 5 percent. A boy born to an unwed mother is 2.5 times more likely to end up in prison than boys raised in two-parent homes.[30]

I am not making excuses for the horrible crimes these men have committed, but place nearly any boy in circumstances with those kinds of disadvantages in life and the likelihood of him ending up in prison is greatly enhanced. Many of the men I speak with did not want to but almost felt destined to end up in prison, as it was all they knew. Most had fathers and grandfathers who were incarcerated. Boys whose fathers are in prison are up to seven times more likely to end up in prison themselves than those who did not have fathers in prison. Most men in prison are shocked when they hear that statistic.

Boys who feel hopeless about their chances to succeed in life are more apt to turn to crime to get their needs met. Also, boys who have negative role models will tend to emulate those examples, even following in the footsteps of crime.

Violence

We are seeing more and more young men in our culture turning to violence as a solution to their frustration and anger. Many of these young men are frustrated by society's failure to engage them and challenge them to anything significant. Others are handicapped by lack of positive male mentors to guide them and the anxiety that abandonment instills in them. Still others fail miserably in our female-dominated educational system and develop feelings of hopelessness, frustration, and anger. Without mentors to teach them to process this angst in a healthy way, or the emotional acumen or the verbal skills to articulate them, many boys lash out, hoping unconsciously to hurt others to deaden the pain they feel. In an effort to "get back" at those who have hurt or humiliated them, they turn to destructive measures when they finally blow up under the pressure of accumulated "stuffed" offenses and assaults to their personhood.

Teen violence is seldom due to one specific cause but is often a combination or accumulation of factors. Phil Chalmers, in his book *Inside the Mind of a Teen Killer*, discusses how a combination of some or all of ten factors contribute to teen violence. He lists the top four as the following: (1) an abusive home life and bullying; (2) violent entertainment and pornography; (3) anger, depression, and suicide; and (4) drug and alcohol abuse.[31] Take a sensitive boy from a broken home who isolates himself and plays too many violent video games, bully him relentlessly at school, then throw some drugs into the mix, and you have a recipe for a young man who eventually gets fed up and lashes out in anger with violence.

Chalmers believes that, while not the sole cause, one of the biggest contributors to teen violence is watching violent movies and playing violent video games. Chalmers currently trains law enforcement personnel on the causes of juvenile homicide. In his book he talks about our boys being so exposed to glorified violence in the media (movies, TV, video games, music) that they are desensitized to it. He says that "violent entertainment and pornography do much more damage to teens than many people are willing to admit. Our teens are bombarded with violent and obscene imagery from a very young age . . . which reaps dangerous consequences."[32] Violent music lyrics like those found in gangsta rap, death metal, and shock rock are just as damaging. Many young people in prison for violent crimes attribute the music they listened to as having a huge influence on their behavior. The American Psychological Association released a study that showed that college students who listen to violent songs were more likely to engage in aggressive behavior and have angry thoughts. Additionally, the American Academy of Pediatrics affirmed that popular music can contribute to depression, suicide, and homicide.[33] This doesn't mean you need to go overboard and start banning every video game on the planet from crossing the threshold of your doorstep. Like most things, violence in video games is subjective and definitely has a differing standard on what boys might consider to be violent versus what moms might consider violent. Games can teach strategic planning skills, hand-eye coordination, problem solving skills, fine motor and spatial skills, and introduction to computers and technology. Many private industry occupations as well as some military positions rely on males who have skills they obtained by playing video games. And games with explosions, destruction, and mayhem are just plain fun. But blowing up planets and spaceships is far different from beheading a human avatar with a sword or disemboweling them with a chainsaw.

Urban gang members without positive male role models develop initiations and rituals involving violence against and even killing other young men. These young men have a skewed perspective on respect and honor, and they are attempting to define masculinity without healthy guidance and training. The reality is that this behavior is not courageous as many of them think. It doesn't take very much bravery to fire an automatic weapon into a crowd of innocent people from a moving car. Nevertheless, violence is the common theme in expressing their frustrations and indignity with life's hopelessness. Boys who are not taught to succeed in life are more prone to use anger and violence to vent their frustrations.

There are many traps designed to keep our young men from fulfilling their destiny. The evil one knows that men and fathers are the key to nearly every problem our culture faces. They are either the cause or the cure. If he can keep men from reaching their potential early in life, he knows he can more easily destroy many other lives as a result. As a mother, your influence can help your son recognize and avoid these traps before the evil one has a chance to use them to get a foothold in his life.

Questions for Reflection and Discussion

1. What kinds of dangers do teenage boys face today?

2. What kinds of cultural influences are young men faced with today?

3. Is school challenging for your son? If so, what are some ways you can help him succeed?

4. Given the easy availability of illegal drugs in middle schools and high schools, how can you teach your son the dangers of experimenting with drugs? Is it important for you as a parent to be educated in the types of abuses taking place in our youth culture?

8

DEVELOPING A
HEALTHY SEXUALITY

*It takes a woman twenty years to make a man of her son,
and another woman twenty minutes to make a fool of
him.*

Helen Rowland

YOUR SON IS now becoming a full-blown sexual being. In
fact, his sexuality will become a big part of who he is
for the rest of his life. He has been created with biological and physical drives geared to propel him forward to
reproduce and propagate the human race. These urges
are extremely powerful and control or at least influence
many of his thoughts and behaviors during adolescence
and throughout his lifetime.

Higher levels of the hormone testosterone and its effects on the male body and psyche create a much higher sex drive in men than in women. God created males like this to perpetuate the species. Not only that, but your son is very interested in sex. If you remember your adolescence, you'll find that your son is probably no different than you were. (Why do we tend to think our kids are different than we were at their age? If anything, kids nowadays are probably much more worldly and sophisticated than we were.)

In *That's My Son* I wrote about your son's impending sexuality. It might be beneficial to reread the chapter on "Boys and Sex," as this chapter builds on content from that book. For teenage boys, the following topics are some things you should be aware of regarding their sexuality.

Girls, Girls, Girls!

By the time your son has entered puberty, he is well aware of the female of our species. He is aware of the young women around him with every aspect of his consciousness. He is alert to how everything he does and says reflects in the perception that females have of him. He is hypersensitive to every female's opinion of him. His body literally forces him to do things geared to draw the attention of the females around him. We call it showing off, but what it is really is nature's way of getting the attention of a female so that he can procreate. Male animals and birds have brightly colored plumage and perform bizarre dances and rituals to attract a mate; young human males get attention by doing outrageous stunts, racing cars recklessly, and performing death-defying acts of skill. Because males of nearly all species invest less in nurturing their offspring than females do, males are genetically predisposed to at-

147

tract as many females as possible to ensure the survival of their bloodline. Females tend to be more selective in choosing a mate. That means the male must expend a large amount of energy attracting the largest pool of candidates possible. So we see young males getting attention by doing provocative and physically dangerous, even crazy activities.

Despite this bravado though, this young male's probably scared to death of girls and confused by the strange power they have over him. Under the best of circumstances females are confusing to males. When hormones are surging through him for the first time, his inexperience around the female gender can be extremely intimidating. It doesn't help that females mature earlier physically, have greater verbal skills, and are much more attuned to their bodies and emotions than males are. Of course most young men bluster and act overly confident in order to cover this fear and feeling of inadequacy. The world of boys requires that they be sexually knowledgeable, unafraid, and show no weakness—especially around girls.

Boys and girls mature at remarkably different rates. Girls are typically two years ahead of boys in physical development, at least until the late teens. Therefore, at least in middle school and early high school, your son is likely to be surrounded by girls who are much more physically and emotionally mature than he is. Without open communication so you can help guide him, he will likely be confused about how girls act and why they are doing the things they do. Unfortunately, due to peer pressure and natural male ego, he cannot refuse the girls' advances. A girl's more aggressive nature in this area can be frightening to a young man who is not as physically developed or emotionally mature as she is. Many young women like to "toy" with boys, learning to use their power in this area. It's a pretty heady experience for a young woman to discover that she has such a powerful ability in the palm of her hand (and other parts of her body).

Because he is wired the way he is (to respond to female sexual advances or opportunities), it is vitally important a boy get from his mother information and training on what constitutes healthy female sexuality. If Mom suffers from unresolved issues due to abuse or other physical, mental, or emotional problems, she may find it difficult to talk to her son about healthy female sexuality. Too often a boy's first sexual encounter comes with a girl who has been wounded, abused, or abandoned by the men in her life. These girls crave masculine affection and often confuse sex for the love they so desperately seek. These experiences are not good for either the young men or the young women.

Cultural Influences

We live in a sex-saturated society. Sex is everywhere—on the internet, in magazines, television, music, movies, and especially in advertising. Nearly half (46 percent) of all fifteen-to-nineteen-year-olds in the United States have had sex at least once.[1] Only 13 percent of fifteen-year-olds have had sex, but by age nineteen about seven out of ten teenagers have engaged in sexual intercourse.[2] The average age of first sexual intercourse is now seventeen. That means by extrapolation that a significant number of teenagers in the church will have also engaged in this behavior long before they are married.

Due to the relaxed moral standards of our culture, the promotion of immoral behavior from the media outlets, and the constant bombardment of sexual images on a daily basis, our young people face a desperate battle to remain sexually pure until marriage.

The lyrics of most popular songs today are incredibly coarse by anyone's standards. Even for a guy like me who has been around the block more than a few times, the lyrics of today's popular music are stunning in their vulgarity. Most are sexually explicit and degrading to females. Again, I am shocked that feminist groups do not protest more regarding the sexual objectification of women in today's music and entertainment industry. I don't want my daughter believing she should conduct herself or think of herself in the terms used for women by popular musicians. And I don't want my son to think about women or treat them as many songs describe. These influences do not teach boys of their responsibility to treat females with honor and respect. They do not encourage them to protect and cherish women as valuable equals.

Our culture is such now that junior high students routinely engage in oral sex (the sixth-grade daughter of my friend recently told him she had been approached by three separate boys at school to have oral sex, including one from her church youth group), trade nude photos of each other in cyberspace, and engage in lewd "grinding" dancing resembling dry sex. High school and college students have a "hook-up" culture called "friends with benefits." This means there is no intimate relationship (or any relationship at all) beyond indulging in sexual intercourse with each other occasionally. One young woman was hurt deeply when during a time of loneliness she contacted her "friend" for support and companionship and was told, "Sorry, ours is just a sexual relationship—there're no strings attached." She finally realized that in this kind of arrangement he was the only friend receiving all the benefits.

This kind of sexual indoctrination has some pretty significant consequences for young people and our culture as well.

Dangers

When I was a teenager in the early 1970s, we only had to worry about two sexually transmitted diseases (STDs)—gonorrhea and syphilis—both of which were easily cured by antibiotics. Neither of those diseases were lifelong or even life-threatening like so many STDs are today. The following are just a few of the consequences associated with promiscuity and premarital sexual activity.

Teen pregnancy is an epidemic in our country. While some statistics show that teen pregnancy rates are down, there are still an estimated 800,000 teen pregnancies every year in this country. Unwanted or unintended teen pregnancy has the consequence of changing a person's entire life (frequently generations of people's lives). Currently, 34 percent of all young women in this country will get pregnant at least once before the age of twenty. Eight out of ten of these pregnancies are unintended, and 81 percent of them are to unmarried teens.[3] Unfortunately, those numbers do not bode well as a predictor for a successful life for a woman or for her children. Just one-third of teen mothers will obtain a high school diploma and only 1.5 percent will get a college degree by the time they are thirty years old.[4] Less than half of all teen fathers finish high school, and those who do are unlikely to seek any higher education.[5]

Many (perhaps most) teen pregnancy situations do not end up happily ever after. According to the Centers for Disease Control, nearly 40 percent (39.7 percent) of all births (1.7 million) in the US are currently out-of-wedlock.[6] Review of a wide variety of studies and books has found that children from single-parent homes are more likely to fall victim to a variety of risk factors (poverty; physical, emotional, and psychological abuse; drug and alcohol usage; early sexual activity and out-of-wedlock childbirth; and crime) that indirectly contribute to lowered educational attainment than children from two-parent biological homes.[7] Children (teens) having children is seldom a good circumstance for the babies or their parents.

Other more lethal consequences to promiscuous sexual behavior loom as an even larger threat. The often fatal AIDS and HIV epidemic in this country and around the world speaks to the dangers of irresponsible sexual activity. In addition, there are a plethora of other sexually transmitted diseases (STDs), several of which are incurable and do great damage to men's and women's bodies. The possible consequences from STDs include infertility, a greater risk for certain types of cancer, brain damage, heart disease, birth defects, and even death.

Approximately one in four sexually active young adults ages fifteen to twenty-four contracts an STD each year. The most common are chlamydia and the human papillomavirus (HPV).[8] The Centers for Disease Control (CDC) estimates 20 million people in the US have HPV. Over 6 million people acquire HPV each year.[9]

The CDC estimates that 35 percent of thirteen-to-nineteen-year-olds are infected with HPV. [10]

Three million cases of chlamydia are reported each year with most STDs occurring in adolescents between the ages of fifteen and nineteen years of age.[11] Genital herpes is also a lifelong disease that is prevalent among sexually active young people.

A study at the University of North Carolina Chapel Hill predicted that one out of two sexually active people between the ages of fifteen and twenty-five will acquire an STD.[12]

The statistics regarding STDs are staggering. It is estimated that 25 percent of sexually active teens currently have an STD or an STI (infection). Many are not aware of it. Basically, *if you sleep with someone, you are sleeping with every person they slept with and every person each of those people has slept with.* You can see how STDs quickly spread exponentially among the population. The only way to ensure that you do not acquire an STD is to practice abstinence. Condoms do not prevent many of the sexual diseases that are rampaging through the community.

Understand too that sexual acts can mean any number of physical acts, each of which can spread STDs. While most adults consider sexual intercourse (vaginal) to be the definition of "having sex," oral, anal, dry sex (humping), and manual (hand-to-organ) manipulation are all sexual activities that can spread STDs. Sex education within the schools often teaches that these activities are safe alternatives to having sexual intercourse.

Sex Education

With all the negative outcomes regarding promiscuous sexuality, it is especially important that our teenagers be properly educated about the dangers involved. But it's difficult talking to your kids about sex. Especially for moms, talking with teenage sons about their sexuality can be a pretty intimidating task. That's why many parents today leave the sexual education of their kids to the schools. Because it's difficult, it's easy to justify putting it aside until it's too late. But because it's tough is precisely why it's our duty as a parent to teach our sons and daughters about sexual purity. Sure it's not easy talking about sex, but even the Bible is pretty straightforward when discussing sexual issues—ever read Ezekiel 23? That chapter is merely a metaphor for Jerusalem, but it's probably just about as shocking to talk to our kids about sex as it is to read these explicit sexual descriptions in the Bible.

The problem with allowing others—like public schools—to educate our children is that their values may not correspond with ours. Jeff Purkiss, author of *Squires to Knights: Mentoring Our Teenage Boys,* relates this alarming example:

> The most alarming issues of the education system are illustrated by the story of Carol Everette. She travels across the country sharing her testimony. She once envisioned a multi-million dollar industry created by her manipulations within the school system. She developed a sex ed curriculum and began teaching it in her local public schools. Her motive: generate future clients for her growing abortion business, ultimately making her rich. She created a business model centered on two things: introduce the minds of elementary students with thoughts of sex while demeaning the authority and credibility of the parents.[13]

The most popular sex education program in public school districts across the country is currently called "Comprehensive Sex Education." Abstinence training has fallen out of favor with a more liberal administration taking over federal funding, and groups like Planned Parenthood have eagerly stepped in to fill the gap. The problem with their philosophy is that even the way they teach abstinence is probably shocking to most parents. One of the more popular curriculums of comprehensive sex education teaches abstinence by having small coed groups of sixth to eighth graders get together and study a list of sexual behaviors such as anal intercourse, mutual masturbation, and oral intercourse to determine a consensus on what *they* consider to be abstinence. It seems very embarrassing and humiliating for a twelve- or thirteen-year-old girl to have to discuss these kinds of activities with a group of boys. Most moms I know wouldn't want their young sons talking about that kind of stuff with girls either.

Another aspect to this program is having students explore the benefits of "Outercourse." This teaches students who want to engage in abstinence to discover the sexual pleasures associated with sexual intercourse without actually engaging in penetration. Their rationale is stated as such: "When young people are making decisions about abstinence, it is important for them to consider not just what their abstinence definition **prohibits** them from doing, but also what it **permits**. . . . when **outercourse** is considered consistent with a person's own definition of abstinence, **most** of the pleasures of sexual intercourse are possible, and much safer"[14] [bold print is in original]. What in the world are supposedly intelligent adults teaching our young children?

I wasn't particularly comfortable talking to my son about sex, much less my daughter. But if you start early and can become comfortable discussing these issues before puberty sets in, you're probably the best person to introduce him to a subject that can be either a friend or a foe throughout his lifetime. He *will* go through puberty and *will* have many questions. Wouldn't you rather your son get the answers to those questions from you than from his buddies down the street—or worse yet, from the secular entertainment industry? Talking about sex early and often while your children are growing up gets them comfortable talking with you about it when it really counts—as they get to be teenagers.

In order to be able to discuss openly with your son God's vision for masculine sexuality, you'll have to develop a strong relationship. This will require *you* reaching out and making the effort to foster a closer relationship. Your son probably won't come to you and initiate discussions about sex.

As a parent, your wisdom and life experience are two of the most valuable contributions you can pass on to your children. The mistakes you've made in this area can help keep your son (or daughter) from making the same mistakes—but not if you don't share them.

Pornography

Porn is part of your son's everyday life. He sees it every day on television, in movies, and on computers. The pornography industry is working hard to catch your son's attention and addict him early in life to their product. The porn industry is a $57-billion-a-year rapidly growing industry—over twice that of McDonald's Corporation. It generates more money than CBS, NBC, and ABC combined, and more than the revenues from professional football, basketball, and baseball combined.[15]

The porn industry spends an incredible amount of money and guile trying to get young people hooked on their product. Because they know that even a glimpse of pornography causes a biological reaction (releases endorphins and adrenaline, which causes a "rush") within

Tools Used by Pornographers

Deception

Porn-napping: purchasing expired domain names when owners forget to renew and redirecting the expired address to porn sites.

Cyber-squatting: using a name that sounds like a legitimate topic (for example, driverslicense.com instead of driverslicense.org).

Misspelling: purposefully buying misspelled domain names for trendy, high-traffic sites.

Advertising: using false error messages, alert boxes, and false forms where one click will open a porn site.

Entrapment

Looping: making a never-ending loop with new porn pages appearing.

Mouse-trapping: altering the use of the back and close buttons so a person is trapped on that site.

Start-up alterations: booting up your computer opens a porn site.

Cookies: placing small files on your computer's hard drive to keep track of every move you make.[16]

the body, they go to great lengths to ensure that children "accidently" catch a glimpse. And once that "rush" happens, it imprints upon the brain a desire for more. For instance, if a child wants to learn about nearly any topic, he can enter it in a website browser and find information. However, if they misspell even just one letter of the word, it can take them to a site that they never intended. Porn distributors do this with nearly all words associated with children and popular topics. If you don't believe me, just test it out on your computer. Because of those efforts, the largest consumer group of pornography is reported to be young men between the ages of twelve and seventeen.

Pornographers consider everyone to fall into one of three categories: targeted, baited, or trapped. They target everyone, even people who aren't looking—especially young people. They bait people by using the strategy described above, in hopes that once those images have been viewed, either curiosity or a desire for that "high" will lead them again to their site. Since porn is highly addictive, once someone becomes addicted they are trapped in a never-ending cycle.

The average age young people admit to being exposed to pornography is between eight and eleven years old. Because males are so visual (especially sexually), pornography is almost irresistibly attractive to them. Pornography is so addictive in the male's mind because it causes a hormone to be released that actually creates a high. It works in the male brain similar to the way cocaine does. This hormone needs greater stimulation and causes the user to need and want more each time it is released. Porn users need bigger prizes, more degrading, more graphic, and more explicit images. The erotic images viewed are cataloged in a male's mind for further use at a later time. They also cause him to be desensitized toward women and to make unfair and unrealistic comparisons.

AWARE, Inc., is an organization in Washington State whose mission is to empower teens by equipping them with the knowledge and strategies for healthy choices regarding sexual activity, encourage parents by providing support and resources to help their children make healthy choices, and equip the community by nurturing a culture that supports abstinence as a healthy choice. They offer a variety of abstinence training programs in schools. They liken the impact of exposing a young man to internet pornography to giving crack cocaine to a baby—addiction is inevitable.[17]

The reality is that pornography degrades women. Pornography makes victims of both the viewer and the one

Effects of Pornography

1. Viewing internet porn and/or engaging in cybersex chat, coupled with masturbation, causes the brain and body to release drugs back into its own nervous system.
2. Based on its ability to produce self-medication, mask pain, escape reality, and provide the means to achieve orgasm, internet porn has been placed in direct competition with illicit drugs.
3. Images viewed for only a few seconds can produce a structural change in the brain and body that may last a lifetime.
4. Pornographic images are stored in cells of the brain and body as cellular memories. These images then become "tangible memories" changing the viewer on the inside.
5. Pornography and sexualized media are teaching teens that sex without responsibility is not only acceptable but even preferable and desirable.[18]

viewed—the only ones who profit are those who sell it. It turns women into objects to be played with, property to be bought and sold. It makes the user think women like rape, torture, and humiliation.

Because males are able to compartmentalize sex, it is vitally important for them to understand that the women in porn are victims, even if willing participants. They need to recognize that those women are someone's daughter and sister and will probably be a wife and mother some day. Many are addicted to drugs, and some are performing against their own will. It is estimated that up to 300,000 young women a year in the US are abducted into human trafficking and sexual slavery. I once spoke at a men's conference where one of the other presenters was a woman who was a former porn star. Her story of how the women in porn movies are abused and victimized was shocking. Her account of the crying and vomiting of women behind the scenes of the movie sets was matched in ferocity only by the universal hatred of men the women possessed.

Pornography is a scourge on the landscape of masculinity. It seems almost irresistible to males because of our visual nature. We are bombarded with sexually graphic images from the time we wake until we go to sleep.

So what can parents do to help protect their son? First of all, keep the door of communication open. Talk with him often about the dangers of pornography and the potential for addiction—just like you would with any other drug. Let him know your opinion of pornography. If he respects you, your opinion will make a difference. If you have reason to suspect that he has been viewing pornography, do not overreact—approach him with respect. Make sure that you monitor activity on the computers in your home and keep them in an area of heavy traffic. Do not let him have a computer in his bedroom. Use a pre-filtered internet system on your computers—Safe Eyes, Net Nanny, and bsecure are just a few software programs that help block internet porn. Check the history files on your computers often. Dig deep because young people know how to change the history. Check CDs, flash drives, and cell phones regularly. Always maintain access to your son's online account and randomly check it. Use parental controls on your computers.

One mom at a seminar told me her tactic, which may be the most effective strategy I have heard of to discourage boys from viewing pornography. She was concerned that her seventeen-year-old son was viewing pornography, so she decided to have a chat with him. She asked if he had noticed that the men and women starring in pornography frequently had "enhanced" anatomical body parts or else were abnormally well-endowed. She then explained that by watching porn, not only would he be disappointed when his future spouse failed to live up to his unrealistic expectations as portrayed in the movies, but what would happen if his young bride had been viewing the same pornography? When she saw him naked for the first time, she might likely respond, "Is that all?" Her son was shocked at that image and probably thought about those consequences more than any other strategy I can think of.

This subject is difficult to talk about and difficult to deal with. But it is worth the effort because of the negative lifelong effects it causes. Make this a priority and a battle to fight.

Masturbation

Without a doubt many people and leaders in the church feel that this is a subject best ignored or denied—at least they act that way. I can't ever remember hearing a sermon about it anyway. And secular society seems to eagerly encourage this activity in young people as a harmless alternative to sexual intercourse. People seem to have a visceral reaction to this topic regardless of whether they are pro or con. Perhaps that's why moms protest loudly whenever I try to cut this topic out of a seminar. Women seem to be extremely interested in a male's perspective on this subject.

As you can imagine, there is probably no topic in the world I would rather avoid discussing in a roomful of women. But it needs to be talked about if for no other reason than because it is so uncomfortable to discuss— that and the fact that it's a pretty ubiquitous activity to everyone walking the face of the earth.

Because of the hormones flooding their bodies, teenage boys are at the height of their sexual prowess by eighteen years old. This causes a tremendous amount of sexual energy and tension to be present in their everyday activities. From that perspective, it may be virtually impossible for a young man not to engage in this activity at least periodically despite his moral background. If that is a realistic assumption, then we can approach this topic from one of two viewpoints: helping our sons deal with it in a healthy manner or one that causes shame and damages a boy's sexual self-image.

Mothers, if not sensitized to the complexities of this issue, can be exceptionally damaging regarding instilling feelings of shame and guilt around this topic. I remember sitting outside shortly after high school graduation with my friend, his mother, and two girls we were dating. His mother unexpectedly made the comment, "I am so glad my son has finally moved out. Now I don't have to deal with the stains on his sheets anymore." Horrified at her insensitivity, her son ran off in shame. The rest of us were shocked at least as much. My friend has never forgiven his mother for that comment, and their relationship is at best strained to this day.

Just like women have a monthly cycle, men also have a cycle. The human male, because of sperm production and other factors, naturally desires sexual release about every forty-eight to seventy-two hours.[19] This desire for release is strong in young males.

Is masturbation harmful physically for a young man? Probably not. Is it unhealthy emotionally especially if it becomes excessive? Probably. Self-gratification that is obsessive (whether it be physically, emotionally, socially, materially, or psychologically) is harmful to an individual. Additionally, narcissism (self-love) is unhealthy for an individual on many levels. Obsession with oneself is unhealthy for relationships and the emotional development of an individual. Self-restraint and delayed gratification teach young men valuable lessons and develop strong character in men. Having the self-discipline to keep oneself strong in this area develops those traits quickly and deeply in a man's character.

Experts on both sides of this issue are divided and each has valid points. Unfortunately, the Bible does not give us any guidance whatsoever on this topic. Yes, there are some passages (such as not lusting after a woman who is not your wife) that could be obliquely applied to this subject, but nothing directly. God did not list in the Ten Commandments, "Thou shalt not masturbate." That certainly would have made this subject much easier to deal with. However, it is hard to believe that an activity that causes us to lust after strangers or those who are not our spouse and that can lead to self-involvement is healthy spiritually.

Maybe the best way for parents to deal with this subject is to talk with their son openly and honestly at an early age (before he is at an age that it becomes an issue) so that he is knowledgeable on the subject. Hopefully your son has a positive male role model in his life to discuss this issue with frequently. Regardless, it should be discussed. Oftentimes activities that are secretive are more attractive.

Sexual Purity

Raising kids to grow up and remain sexually pure until marriage seems like a daunting, if not impossible, task. But the rewards of making this a priority are abundant to your son and even to our culture.

Some moms misunderstand their son's sex drive, still thinking of him as a little boy. One woman during a seminar asked if it was okay for her seventeen-year-old son to be in his bedroom with his girlfriend with the door closed—even though the parents were home. When I told her no, she had a little trouble understanding my reasoning. I finally said, "Would you let your husband spend hours alone behind closed doors in your bedroom with a young attractive woman? Even if you were home?"

After a moment of stunned silence, she and every other woman in the room answered with a resounding "No!"

I replied, "Then what's the difference between your son and your husband?" I think she understood my point after that.

When young males are forced to delay their sexual gratification, it develops aspects of their psyche as well as increases their respect for a woman. As part of the natural maturation process, young men who are forced (or better yet, voluntarily make that choice) to wait to satisfy their sexual urges develop a number of positive qualities that don't occur when they are given easy and early sexual gratification. Some of these growth patterns are on a physiological level and some are on a psychological level. The main point though is that young men who are forced to wait develop quality character traits.

Part of our role as parents is to protect teenagers from adolescent sex until they can acquire the skills of adulthood before taking on the responsibilities of marriage and parenthood.

One way to help your son with his sexual challenges is to keep him occupied—especially with physical activities. This tends to take the edge off the lustful urges and desires that all men have, but especially adolescent boys. Part of the purpose of staying active and stimulating your mind and body is to ward off boredom. When a male is feeling challenged mentally and physically, and has significance in his life, he feels secure, fulfilled, and good about himself. This leaves less time and energy for boredom and contemplating the lack of adventure. This lack of adventure is the downfall of many a male's sexual purity. Too often males use sex as a substitute cure for poor self-esteem or boredom or for not doing anything significant with their lives. I believe one of the factors that contributes to higher out-of-wedlock birth rates in urban inner cities is the hopelessness that permeates the culture. Without the ability or anticipation of being able to get a high-paying, prestigious job, the only way for a young man to prove his manhood is by having sex with as many girls as possible.

Another way to help your son remain sexually pure is by helping him set boundaries. Again there is a fine line between encouraging your teen son to develop critical decision-making skills and still enforcing the rules of your home. Teens are acutely aware of the image they project to the world. One way to help them think through the decisions they make is to ask them, "How old do you think that decision would make you look?" or "What would you think about someone who made a decision like that?" It is easier to set boundaries in advance so we have a set of guidelines in place *before* we find ourselves in a situation where they are tested. Males in particular are doomed to fail in this area if they do not have a preexisting commitment and accountability.

Your son needs to understand the responsibility that he holds in his hands. He now has the ability to create life—not a responsibility to take lightly. It is important that he think about that and understand that if he creates life, even though the laws of this country say it is a

165

woman's choice, he will still be held accountable by God for what happens to that life. It is a sobering realization that we are responsible for a life we created. I encourage you to have many discussions with him about the ramifications of engaging in sexual activity irresponsibly. Even though I believe abstinence until marriage is the way God has best designed us to live our lives, nearly every other portion of our society shouts at him that engaging in premarital sex is fun, healthy, and does not have any negative consequences—and besides, everyone else is doing it.

Part of setting boundaries for ourselves is then having accountability in our lives to help enforce them. Most males, even those with sterling self-control and moral integrity, are not capable of resisting temptation without some form of accountability. The truth is, without being held accountable, many males will not even live up to their responsibilities in life.

Accountability makes all the difference in the world when it comes to a male being sexually responsible. For instance, I'm careful to make sure that I have other people to whom I am accountable at every seminar I present to women. Not because I am so desirable personally, but because I *represent* what many of these women yearn for in life. Hence, it's important that I take the proper precautions to ensure that I have accountability at all times so I'm not tempted to take advantage of someone's vulnerability. Males are naturally equipped to instinctively know when a woman is either vulnerable or available. Even when it's not obvious, we often can sense an opportunity. It explains why some women just seem to have men flock around them, even when they are not overtly sensuous or even necessarily that attractive.

When a man walks without accountability in his life, he tends to make up the rules as he goes—he has a tendency to justify or rationalize whatever desires his mind comes up with. It's a lesson that boys need to learn early in life.

Encourage your son to recognize the importance of accountability and then to set up a structure that works for him. Young men who are empowered to work through these issues themselves are more apt to abide by them better than those who have boundaries forced upon them by others. Help and encourage your son to make a decision on what his sexual boundaries and limits are and then share them with you, his father, or better yet a group of his close friends. If he writes them down as a contract with himself, it might be even more binding.

From puberty forward, sex now plays a huge factor in your son's life. Take time to make developing a healthy sexuality a priority in your parenting. It's important because it is such a big part of his life, for the rest of his life, from this day forward.

Questions for Reflection and Discussion

1. Some moms refuse to believe their little boys are becoming men. Have you started to recognize your son's sexuality yet?

2. Why do teenage boys do crazy stunts?

3. In your opinion, does our culture promote a healthy or unhealthy view of sexuality to our young people? Why or why not?

4. Are you aware of the number and widespread infection level of STDs (sexually transmitted diseases) in our country?

5. Have you started educating your son about sex or are you relying on schools and other sources to teach him?

6. What can parents do to stop the epidemic of pornography from "steamrolling" young men?

9

SPIRITUAL LEGACY

Of Gods and Monsters

*I remember my mother's prayers and they have always
followed me. They have clung to me all my life.*

Abraham Lincoln

YOUNG PEOPLE REFLECT the values of their family. The
character of the relationship with their family of origin
strongly affects their spiritual journey. Those values are
the foundation they build their lives upon. Values contribute to the philosophy and worldview we live our lives
by. Young men who do not get a spiritual foundation early
in life often struggle with the choices and decisions they
make. Without a compass to steer them and guide their
choices, they founder like a ship without a rudder.

169

One of the laments I hear from the men in prison is that they had no spiritual training while growing up. They didn't know what they didn't know. No one took the time to teach them the values that a spiritual upbringing produces in a young man. Clearly these men can see where lack of a value system harmed their lives. They do not have a foundation that gives them guidelines to make decisions with or to live their lives by.

The teen years are those years when a young man's mind is expanding and the concepts of right and wrong, good and evil, and sacrifice and selfishness are finally starting to be understood. This is the time when he can start grasping complicated concepts such as religion and faith. Dr. Randall Eaton says, "Adolescence also is the sensitive period for the awakening of spiritual life and acquisition of wholeness."[1] But too often we lose our boys and young men just when they are finally capable of understanding what true faith really looks like.

Why Teen Boys Leave the Church and How to Bring Them Back

The truth is, even young men raised in the church are leaving in droves. And those who have not been raised in the church are not too interested in finding out about it. As so very clearly pointed out in David Kinnaman's book *unChristian*, Christianity has a real perception problem with young people today—both those inside and outside the church. They believe Christians are judgmental, anti-gay, anti-choice, angry, violent, illogical empire builders who want to convert everyone else.[2] Peer pressure and the tenets of a relativistic culture that elevates acceptance, diversity, inclusion, and tolerance as the highest virtues attainable make the absolute truths of Christianity seem outdated, backward, and foolish. The only "truths" of our culture are the merits of multiculturalism and the god of the environment (oh yes, and that animals are equal to human beings). And of course if Dad does not provide a model of attending church and living a godly lifestyle, the possibility of a boy staying in church diminishes rapidly in correlation to his age.

But men aren't too excited about church either, it appears. Contemporary authors such as David Murrow, John Eldredge, and Paul Coughlin have all recently pointed out the flaws of the church in attracting and keeping males, especially young males. They very accurately attribute this to the overwhelming feminization of the church in America that has marginalized and even repelled most men.

Males seem to struggle more with developing a deep, spiritual relationship with God than women do. I'm not sure if it's a pride issue, the common "do it yourself" attitude of most men, or just plain apathy. I do know most men don't really seek God until a crisis affects their life. And many abandon that relationship after the crisis passes.

The typical man who does attend church is expected to be "humble, tidy, dutiful, and above all else, nice."[3] Good traits in a man, but not to the exclusion of or at least balanced by more masculine traits such as passion, action, conviction, and achievement. Murrow says that while males have not completely abandoned the church, manly men have all but disappeared. As he says, "Tough, earthy, working guys rarely come to church. High achievers, alpha males, risk takers, and visionaries are in short supply. Fun-lovers and adventurers are also underrepresented in church. These rough-and-tumble men don't fit in with the quiet, introspective gentlemen who populate the church today."[4]

To be fair, not all men who attend church are milque-toasts. I have spoken at and attended churches that liter-ally vibrated with healthy masculinity (these are usually larger, growing churches with dynamic manly pastors). Frankly, I think my buddies and I are as manly a men as ever walked the face of the earth and we all attend church. And most of the men who attend the men's conferences that I speak at in the US and Canada are strong examples of healthy masculinity. But the truth is that most men in church are either uninvolved or so passive that they are repugnant to the average guy. One nonbelieving young man told me, "I have been to many churches and met a lot of really nice guys while there. But they all struck me as being guys who wouldn't even defend their wives if they needed to. I don't want to hang around guys like that." That is a sad indictment of men in the church. Any wonder why our boys are not inspired by this model of Christian masculinity?

Why Teen Boys Need Men in Church

Boys and young men are drawn to action, adventure, com-petitiveness, achievement, and even conflict. Men were created in the image of God, and Jesus came to earth as a man. However, the image the church has projected of Jesus is one of meekness, gentleness, kindness, humility, and even weakness. Our popular depiction of Jesus as *only* the Lamb of God—meek and mild—does a disservice to boys who are repelled by that feminized image. Not only that but we do a disservice to Jesus himself, who was the epitome of masculinity. Jesus was no sissy. While Jesus *was* humble, loving, kind, and forgiving with those who needed it, he was more often than not causing conflict. He was a man of action when need be. He was confrontational, opinionated, and often exasperated by the stupidity of his followers. He was intelligent, shrewd, and a passionate and inspiring orator. His language was often coarse, sarcastic, and disrespectful toward government officials and church leaders. He engaged in unacceptable behaviors and hung around with people (prostitutes, beggars, and drunkards) who were considered undesirable by good church folks. Besides knocking over tables and brandishing a whip in a rage to drive a whole room of money-changers out of the temple, he ticked people off enough that they wanted to stone him on more than one occasion and even throw him off a cliff (in his own hometown, no less). He did not avoid conflict but seemed to go out of his way to challenge the Pharisees and the Sadducees as well as magicians, idolators, scribes, and legalistic church leaders whenever possible. He eventually willingly gave his life in bloody, brutal fashion for the benefit of all humankind.

Besides being demeaning, the Nancy-boy image of Jesus only tells half the story—it leaves out the part that would appeal most to boys. The picture of a soft, gentle, androgynous-looking pretty boy is not only distasteful to boys, it is false. First of all, he was probably dark skinned (he probably did not have blue eyes) and had a weather-beaten face from working outdoors in the hot sun. Jesus was raised a carpenter by trade back when there were no power tools. Carrying heavy logs from the shipyard, lifting and splitting them, sawing them by hand, and pounding nails, day in and day out, would have developed a rough-hewn, muscular physique with strong, well-calloused hands. Because of the nature of his work, the climate, and the level of hygiene customs practiced at the time, he was probably sweaty and dirty most of the time and might have even had strong body odor. He probably cut himself or smashed his finger with a hammer occasionally (although I doubt he responded the same way I do to those events) and had gnarled hands and fingers. In short, if Jesus truly was God in the form of man (which the Bible says he was), then he probably had all the traits and behaviors of any other man.

The pale, skinny, timid, domesticated image we have projected of the Savior of the world is false and repels most boys. Here's how Coughlin says it: "Here's our popular misconception: Jesus didn't drink, swear, get angry, use sarcasm, confront, avoid questions, grow impatient, or complain. Conversely, the record shows he did all of the above, and the gospel includes *no* apology, confession, or repentance for any of them."[5]

A male initially gets his faith by being vulnerable enough to risk humbling himself before God. Faith then develops through the difficult times and grows experientially. Faith is a gift from God that can grow based on experience and testimony. I like the saying that faith is spelled "RISK"! God also grows a man's faith through suffering. The same fire that hardens clay melts wax. A true believer who suffers will run *to* God rather than run *from* God. What I have found is that as I go through times when I feel overwhelmed and cry out to God, he shows himself to me in new ways I hadn't expected: through the Word of God, people, or the circumstance I am in.

Safe churches do not allow a boy to test himself and grow in his faith. Enjoying risk-taking is a uniquely male condition, and boys who are not allowed to take risks in church look for them elsewhere. The opportunity to take risks also contributes to the growth of our faith. My faith has grown immensely during the past five years in which I have stepped out in faith in full-time ministry. Taking that risk and having to rely on God has matured and deepened my faith. I know men who never risk anything and thus have a shallow faith.

Older male figures are especially important to developing the spirituality of boys and young men. Rare is the man who develops faith apart from the influence of other men. It is seldom an intellectual exercise but is more often nurtured by men he respects. Part of the problem is the "image" projected of Christian masculinity. What man or boy wants to be like some of the big-hair guys on TV? Finding other Christian men he can be comfortable with allows him to emulate them and be mentored by them.

I frequently speak at Promise Keepers Canada events where hundreds of dads bring their sons or fatherless young men. The boys and young men are excited, inspired, and passionate when the speakers light a fire in their belly by teaching them the true value of Christian masculinity and manhood modeled after Jesus Christ.

Young males in particular desire opportunities to apprentice under an older man. These relationships are frequently those of a mentor in nature and may be just as important or even more so than those with a relative. As with most things, a young adult male must see an older male modeling a spiritual walk in order to "get it." The key is finding other Christian men he can be comfortable with, which then allows him to emulate them and be mentored by them. If he sees only passive, timid, weak men in the church, he will not find men he looks up to and wants to be like.

Young men are bored with church, and teenage and college-aged males are leaving the church in droves. Frankly, I even struggle with finding a church that satisfies all my needs. I understand that many pastors contend the church's job is to teach the Word of God, but I want a church that is on the edge, that's growing and reaching out to the hurting in the community—a hospital for sinners. I want to be part of something exciting and significant— that makes a difference in the world. I don't want to come every Sunday and sit in the same seat, looking at the same people who dress alike and look alike, hearing the same message by the same people over and over again. It is my opinion that the church is doing a disservice to men, especially young men, by abandoning them. If the church does not change the way it does "business," we will lose a whole generation of young people, eventually becoming a post-Christian nation as has happened in countries throughout Europe. America may become a nation filled with beautiful but empty cathedrals dotting the landscape.

Or perhaps we are already there.

Why Males Struggle with Church

One area that we need to be aware of in Christian manhood is the propensity toward behavior-based performance. Many men and boys I know have the attitude that "if *all* God is interested in is how I behave, then I'm not very interested in God." Because men and boys cannot live up to those perfect expectations, many men in these circumstances either give up or fake it—which might be worse. Unfortunately, those "perfect expectations" often come from other men (church leaders), not from God, who knows we are not capable of meeting that standard. Holy behavior is important and has its place in a man's spirituality, but "behavioral Christianity" lacks depth and is not attractive to most men. We have enough pressure to perform every day without being expected to attain unrealistic expectations of holiness.

Churches and church leaders that promote a message of guilt, shame, and self-incrimination browbeat males into cowardice and passivity. These types of churches use a legalistic, performance-based agenda that most men cannot live up to. Their legalism is a "collection of beliefs predicated on a notion that if we follow a certain variety of very specific disciplines, we will receive God's approval and secure his blessings and their related rewards."[6] This includes a list of do's and don'ts that change from one church or denomination to another, with increasingly greater expectations to obtain acceptable piety.[7]

More than performance-based theology, young men need to be inspired by the thrills and adventure that come from living life on the edge, walking with God, and living the life he inspires men toward. So many men in the Bible were incredibly powerful examples of masculinity and lived fantastic, unbelievable adventures. These examples teach valuable life lessons to boys. Jonah (although probably not the best example of masculinity) was swallowed at sea by a giant fish and vomited back up on shore—how cool would that be. Daniel survived being thrown in a hungry lion's den because of his faith. Shadrach, Meshach, and Abednego lived and were unharmed despite being tossed into a fiery furnace so hot that it killed the guys standing outside. Joshua and Caleb ventured into unexplored lands containing giants and yet came back excited about the prospect of entering into war with them.

Joseph survived and prospered despite being sold into slavery by his brothers and being wrongly accused of rape. His is a good example of always doing the right thing for the right reason and not having good immediate results. However, this was not failure but faithfulness and was honored by God.

Samson once killed a thousand men with the jawbone of a donkey and yet was rendered impotent by his poor choices with women. Perhaps the most manly man in the Bible, David, killed a nine-foot-tall giant with a bad attitude, all with just a rock and a sling when he was a teenager. Prior to that he had killed both a lion and a bear with his bare hands—and he was just a boy! David inspired such powerful and mighty warriors to follow him that several of them had each killed 300 men at one time by themselves. And yet David was all too human. He committed murder, adultery, and was by all accounts a poor father and husband. Yet because of his faith and repentant attitude, God favored David and called him a man after his own heart. It's a powerful lesson in that God often values our faith more than our performance.

These are the messages of masculinity that attract boys. Adventure, mighty battles (Jonathan and his page killing thirty men by themselves), trials and tribulations, good versus evil, Jesus performing miracles—these are the stories that inspire boys and attract them to a life worth living.

A Mother's Role

If that is all true, then how does a mother help inspire her teenage son to continue forward in his faith? Many a mom has taken her son to church his entire childhood only to be devastated when he fell away from the church in his teens and twenties. Not only that, but passing on a spiritual legacy to our children is difficult. Our children have a way of finding the flaws in our own spirituality. Most of us probably feel like the parents of the little boy in this story:

> After the christening of his baby brother in church, Jason sobbed all the way home in the back seat of the car. His father asked him three times what was wrong. Finally, the boy replied, "That preacher said he wanted us brought up in a good Christian home, and I wanted to stay with you guys."

Mothers are extremely important during the early childhood years in instilling a spiritual foundation in their sons. There's an old Spanish proverb that says an ounce of mother is worth a ton of priest. Her dedication and faith are a strong example to a boy. Most men credit their mother with teaching them spiritual faithfulness and commitment. A boy wants to please her and for the most part will (if not somewhat reluctantly) attend church with her. However, as he gets older, the boredom and feminine message of church start to wear him down. And if Dad stays home and watches the game on TV instead of attending church, Mom will start finding it more and more difficult to drag the kids to church on her own as they get older. Here are some tips to help your son like church long enough to develop his own faith.

Start developing your son's faith early in life. Even though my daughter appeared to reject the Christian walk during her turbulent teenage years, she has come back and realizes the value of having God in her life. This is because it was what was taught to her at a young age. My son is now college age, and while he appears somewhat ambivalent about his faith walk, he too recognizes the fundamental truths about God and his salvation. I fully anticipate that he will once again lead a godly life as he gets older and starts a family, especially as I continue to model authentic faith.

Another area to be aware of is how you present your faith to your son. For example, if you live out a life of godly service in humility and faith, your son will internalize those values. If, however, you live a hypocritical spiritual life where you look good on the outside but criticize and complain about others and never do anything to serve others outside the doors of the church, you will pass that attitude on to your son. If you have never risked anything for your faith, your son has probably never seen God answer your prayers.

Understand also that males learn best from object lessons. For example, Albert Einstein once described relativity by saying, "When a man sits with a pretty girl for an hour, it seems like a minute. But let him sit on a hot stove for a minute—and it's longer than any hour. That's relativity."[8] With that in mind, look for everyday examples or situations from your past where you can openly and honestly share your faith and how God has worked in your life. Don't be afraid to let your son know you made mistakes. Our kids know we are not perfect, and so telling him where you have struggled in life and why God's presence was helpful is very important. One of the blessings of being in full-time ministry is that God is faithful to show me and our children the fruits of my labor on a nearly daily basis. It is hard to argue with the concrete facts and reality of God's actions. My wife has a propensity to turn many things into lectures. But sometimes less is more, and actions always speak louder than words. Our example of living a godly life is a much more powerful message than any lecture could ever be.

Next, seek a church that has *healthy* masculine leadership—not a masculine-dominated church or a feminized one. It should have a balance between female leadership and male contribution. If all of the leadership (except the senior pastor) of the church, volunteers, ministry programs, and program directors are geared toward or led by women, then the church probably has a feminine spirit. Your son needs to see men living out a faith-based lifestyle. He needs to be around them and see how they deal with life's struggles and the value they place on their spirituality. If that is not modeled for him by a man or other men, it will be difficult for him to grasp the concept and to place much value upon it.

Look for books and movies that portray men of valor who were (or are) Christians and fought for a noble cause. Throughout history, the men who accomplished the greatest deeds were followers of Christ. In fact, studying the lives of great men throughout history, and finding they all had the common thread of being Christians, is what ultimately led me to accepting Christ into my heart. Explain the connection between these men's faith and the life of significance they led. Christ calls us to greatness, but many of us fail to answer the call. Young men yearn for greatness.

Look for manly men who are doing things of significance for your son to hang around with. One church I know has a "Hot Rod" ministry where a group of men purchase an old beat-up car or truck. They then meet every Saturday for a year to fix it up into a hot rod. They invite sons and fatherless boys to join them, working side by side. At the end of the year, they have a huge celebration festival where they auction off the hot rod and then use the profits to buy another "junker" to start all over again. Many men's ministries have programs that work on cars or do home repairs for single moms. This allows your son to see men using their skills for the benefit of those in need. Any time you can get your son (or daughter) to take the focus off himself and redirect it toward helping those less fortunate than him, it is a powerful life lesson.

Other churches take boys on annual hunting or fishing trips. Some of the best times I've had in church with my son were going to men's retreats where we went whitewater rafting, gun shooting, and rock climbing. Mix that day of activities in with a powerful message from a manly pastor and the thundering sound of a hundred men worshiping together and you've got a winning strategy to capture the heart of a boy.

Encourage your husband or other men in the church to start discipleship groups such as Robert Lewis's *Raising a Modern-Day Knight* or Men's Fraternity, or John Eldredge's *Wild at Heart Field Manual* and include teenage boys in the group. Boys and young men love studying and learning alongside older men who are being honest and vulnerable. Teenage boys crave authenticity, so these kinds of groups can be very powerful in shaping the heart of a young man.

Another area you need to be aware of is the influence of outside sources in your son's spiritual walk. One of the idiosyncrasies I observed by attending graduate school as an adult was the propensity for university professors to teach their *opinion* to easily influenced young people instead of teaching facts. To truly educate college students, they should be given both sides of an issue in an unbiased fashion and then encouraged through debate, research, and careful consideration to determine what their opinion is on the subject. This is known as critical thinking—a commodity in ever-shrinking, short supply in our country's students. Too much of what is taught in college is filtered through the professor's worldview and the political bent of the university. Most of higher academia is secular, if not ultraliberal, in nature.

If your son plans to attend college, help prepare him by teaching him not to rely on only one person or source for information, no matter the subject. When I research a topic to write a book, I look at information from a variety of sources; I read dozens of books from both Christian and secular authors on the subject. I review information from a number of sources and then glean what I believe to be true and relevant from those sources and discard the rest. It is also important to teach your son to look at the agenda behind what an individual or entity proposes. This helps determine the validity of their information.

Many, if not most, students who attend college at least temporarily walk away from their faith. Part of the reason is the agenda and worldview they are subjected to by the university and upper academia. I attended a Christian graduate school and yet was openly mocked and chastised by fellow students and the professor for suggesting that the theory of evolution was just a *theory*. Somehow the concept of keeping an open mind had been filtered out of them to the degree that they couldn't accept anything outside their "box." Just because something is thought to be true and promoted by the reportedly most intelligent people in the land does not necessarily mean it is true. It wasn't long ago that university professors and scientists thought the world was flat and that the way to cure sickness was by bloodletting. Anyone who disagreed with those beliefs was mocked and ridiculed—similar to today.

183

If your son is to hang on to his faith and belief system as he goes out into the world, it will be important that you instill in him the ability to look at the information given him with an open mind and use critical-thinking skills to determine whether that information is actually fact, theory, or someone's opinion. Instead of arguing with him, challenge him at every opportunity to look at things from all possible angles and perspectives. Encourage him to look at the agenda behind the information and who or what other organizations believe in and support that information.

Finally, pray for your son every day. Pray for his spiritual, emotional, physical, and psychological health and safety. Pray God would bring healthy mentors and good friends into his life. Pray for his sexual purity. Pray for his future spouse (and her parents). Pray for wisdom and discernment. And pray for your son's decision making. My wife prayed daily that our children would get "caught." She knew that they *would* make mistakes and poor choices, but if they got caught the first time they did something wrong, it would prevent them from harm or continuing until the consequences were serious. I believe God answered those prayers as our teens were continually baffled that they always got caught whenever they strayed from the path.

These are just a few examples of how you can encourage your son's faith. Ultimately, our children have to come to a place where they develop their own faith. They have to get out from under their parents' faith and find their own relationship with God. If you have modeled a genuine relationship with the Lord, your children will be much more likely to understand and feel the need and importance of a relationship for themselves.

However, even if your teenage or young adult son walks away from his faith, do not lose hope. Many young men do step away from the church and come back later. Again, your example of loving them instead of judging them is an important model of Christian faith. Loving them does not mean you are condoning their decision or choices, but it does mean that you care enough to keep the relationship open. Your son's spiritual salvation is an area that is too important to close the doors on.

Questions for Reflection and Discussion

1. Is spiritual training important for young men? If you are a Christian or belong to another religion, your answer is probably yes. But what if you are not a religious person—is spiritual training important? Why or why not?

2. Why are young men leaving the church? If you attend church, have you noticed a lack of high school and college-aged young men in attendance?

3. Why might boys and young men be put off by the traditional image projected by the Christian church of Jesus?

4. How can a mother help her son develop his faith? How might she harm his development?

10

BUILDING CHARACTER
FOR A LIFETIME

Children have never been very good at listening to their elders, but they never failed to imitate them.

James Baldwin

THE ONLY THING that a man has in this world that cannot be taken from him is his character. Boys and men without character never fulfill their potential in life. But in the postmodern culture we live in that does not believe in absolute truths, morals (although they do promote situational ethics), or the existence of right and wrong, how do we teach our sons the importance of character?

One thing we must remember is that our children will always imitate what we *do*, not what we *say* to do. Unfortunately, they always seem to imitate our worst traits instead of our best. Because of that tendency, we need to constantly be aware of the example of character we set for them.

When our children were eight and ten years old, we took a vacation to Puerto Vallarta, Mexico. One day we decided to take a guided snorkeling cruise. Unbeknownst to me, as is the custom on these cruises, the crew of the boat was plying the male tourists with tequila "shooters." Because I seldom drink alcohol anyway (especially at nine o'clock in the morning), I was refusing their offers even though the rest of the men on board were steadily accepting the free refreshments. Perhaps the crew considered my refusals a challenge because they stepped up their efforts to get me to take a drink. They became quite aggressive, even going so far as to "jokingly" question my manhood. Frankly, after a while of steady pressure, they started to wear me down, and I thought to myself, "What the heck, I'm on vacation. What's wrong with taking one drink?"

Fortunately, as I was just about to cave in, I looked around and saw two sets of little round, wide eyeballs watching me intently. Given that my wife and I had been spending the better part of their childhood telling them the merits of resisting peer pressure, it didn't seem like a good time to demonstrate just the opposite in front of my kids, and so I firmly refused any further attempts to solicit me with libations. I shiver to think that one moment of weakness on my part could have ruined all the hard efforts we had made to teach them a valuable character trait. Had they witnessed my succumbing to peer pressure, nothing I would have said on the subject would have counted after that. Perhaps nothing I would have said on any subject after that would have carried much merit.

Our sons need to be taught a value system if they are to grow up strong and healthy and fulfill their important roles in life as men. They need to be taught a well-defined set of ideals. Character is the most important ingredient in a healthy, authentically masculine man. Masculine strength needs to be refined by sterling character. Our character foundation is what allows us to most resemble that depiction. If our sons are not taught a value system by their parents they will likely adopt one that is modeled for them by another person or segment of society.

Author Aubrey Andelin considers character to be the most important element in a man's value system. He comments that Shakespeare "depicts perfect manhood as being *in action like an angel, in appearance like a god*."[1] Andelin didn't quite get the quotation right. Here it is, from Hamlet: "What a piece of work is man! how noble in reason! how infinite in faculty! in form and moving how express and admirable! in action how like an angel! in apprehension how like a god! the beauty of the world, the paragon of animals!"[2]

The truth is, if your sons don't learn their value system from you, they will learn it from someone—probably someone you won't appreciate. We know that corporate America, Madison Avenue, the mainstream media, and the music and entertainment industries all deny any culpability in influencing our children. And for the sake of profit are actually *willing* to morally corrupt our children at ever earlier ages.

At least one popular rap star has publically stated that he is not a role model despite the fact that he is idolized by millions of young men. And in response to the potential negative effects of his violent video game (which is banned in Australia because it is so violent) on young people, he denied culpability by stating, "A person who is influenced by a video game is already so damaged that they are dangerous."[3] Other music performers admit to an agenda of intentionally morally corrupting the youth of today. Part of this may be an act to garner publicity, but they seem pretty convincing to me. Either way the effects on impressionable youth with less than fully developed critical-thinking skills and decision-making processes are still highly deleterious. It is important to remember that teens are not little adults—they are actually closer mentally and emotionally to big children. That means they *are* influenced by the people they look up to and want to emulate.

Even the public education system is ambiguous at best regarding teaching ethics and character to young people. I recently heard this story from a schoolteacher who was involved in this process. A public high school wanted to update their school motto and choose something that would inspire the students to be proud of their school. They put the message to a vote of the student body and asked them which words they wanted to have as their school motto. The students overwhelmingly chose the words "Glory, Honor, and Strength" as the words that best represented them and also fit the acronym of their school initials. Later, during a staff meeting to discuss the results of the survey and how best to implement them, the majority of the teachers refused to approve those three words as the school slogan. They felt those words were not "inclusive" of all and were not worthy of promotion. In fact they considered them to be somewhat offensive. One counselor stated with disgust, "How are you supposed to teach traits like honor anyway?" Interestingly, Martin Luther King Jr. (a man the public education system claims to admire) felt just the opposite about this issue when he said, "The function of education is to teach one to think intensively and to think critically. Intelligence *plus character*—that is the goal of true education" (italics mine).[4]

The teenage years are a time when other adults and peers become more influential to a young person than his parents. However, while parents think they have less influence, they are still in fact the most important factor in the foundation of a teenager. The character traits modeled by the adults who influence your son's life are likely the traits he will think are noble and worthy of aspiring toward. My former high school principal had a saying, "What you permit you promote." Your son needs to know—even now more than ever—what you believe in and *why*.

Listed below are just some of the character traits that I think young men need to be taught and why. You can find more examples of healthy masculine character traits described in my books *Better Dads, Stronger Sons* and *The Power of a Man*. Consider what you think is important and then develop a plan to teach your son what you want to promote. The following are only a few of the character traits we should strive to proactively teach our sons. I have tried to give some examples of how this can be achieved plus why it is necessary for boys to learn these traits.

Resiliency

> Strength and honor!
>
> Maximus Decimus Meridius, *Gladiator*

One way that boys learn successful life skills is through being taught resiliency. Resiliency is the ability to bounce back quickly from trials or tragedy. It keeps men from giving up when the going gets tough. Resiliency is part of the "heart" of a man.

Boys learn resiliency by being pushed to excel, especially by older males. All of my high school sports coaches made a big impact on my life. In particular, I can remember my old high school track coach, Max Jensen. I doubt Coach Jensen was a Christian man, but his constant exhortations to force myself to exceed my perceived self-limitations taught me resiliency, self-discipline, perseverance, and the value of hard work. All my coaches, especially football and wrestling, used whatever means necessary—including but not limited to physical punishment, taunting and verbal challenging, or praise—to teach me character strengths. They pushed me to succeed beyond what I believed I was capable of. I am a better man today because of it. But disciplinarian coaches like that are rare today, whether it be in high school, college, or the pros. Young men are not taught respect for authority or to value self-discipline and hard work. They suffer their entire lives because of it.

As an example, military boot camps are designed to break young men down and teach them to work together as a team. They use sometimes harsh discipline and extreme measures to get young men to see that they are capable of exceeding their expectations. They do this because they know the traits of self-discipline and resiliency in a man can save his life and all the other lives in his platoon.

Boys who do not learn self-discipline and resiliency often get into trouble with the law. Only through desperate measures can we bring them back from the brink of destruction. By way of illustration, I recently watched an incredibly inspiring video. The Palm Beach County, Florida, Sheriff's Office operates a five-month school and boot camp called Eagle Academy (www.pbso.org/eagle academy/). It is specifically designed for at-risk kids between the ages of thirteen and sixteen. These young people have all previously struggled or been in serious trouble before voluntarily entering the program. The program on the video appeared to be very similar to my recollections of military boot camp, consisting of daily physical training, education, and character training. Most of the young men in the video came from an undisciplined environment, many from single-parent homes where their mothers constantly indulged them. It was marvelous to watch these angry young men first resist and even hate the boot camp but then bloom under the guidance and coaching of older men who pushed them beyond their comfort zone to learn character traits such as respect, perseverance, and teamwork. After garnering the boys' respect and motivating them, the drill instructors (DIs) quickly turned into mentors and coaches of life skills. There were even several female DIs, which taught the boys to respect women (something they desperately needed to learn). While their sons were in the program, parents received weekly counseling on parenting skills as well.

The boys had high expectations placed upon them during the camp, many for the first time in life, and they blossomed under those expectations. They were strictly held accountable for the consequences of their decisions and choices. After teaching the boys the definition of respect, the drill instructors worked on improving their self-esteem by making them overcome challenges they were afraid of, such as rappelling off a ninety-foot tower. Accomplishing achievements they did not think they could do gave them a true, healthy self-esteem instead of the false self-esteem promoted by a culture that encourages false praise, egalitarianism, and lowered expectations. The program also brought in the best educators available, and most of the boys claimed that the school portion was their favorite part of the program. Many were succeeding in an educational environment for the first time in their lives. It was exciting to watch them enjoy learning instead of hating school.

The final challenge of the program before graduation was an exercise designed to push them beyond their limits both physically and emotionally. It was a twenty-four-hour period of physically challenging obstacle courses combined with mental toughness exercises. For instance, the boys were challenged (they chose of their own free will) to sit in tubs of ice water at midnight after participating in exhausting physical exercises all day and night. They were kept continually wet and made to roll in the sand, which was incredibly irritating and mentally exhausting after a long period of time. Every activity was designed to push them beyond the limits of what they thought they could endure. It taught them that they were capable of enduring hardships beyond what they thought possible—it taught them to be resilient. Now when life throws them a curve ball, they will not be as likely to give up. When any of the students did quit the challenge course, they were treated with compassion and encouragement by the drill instructors. These young males were literally transformed from boys into men in five months just by a few older men coaching, mentoring, and pushing them to become all they were capable of. The program was difficult, but by the end the boys loved the camp and were very proud of themselves for having completed the program.

I don't know what the success rate of this program is, but I have to believe that being proactive in the lives of these boys saved many of them from a destiny of hopelessness and despair. Obviously, you cannot determine how many of the boys who have gone through the program are not in prison today that might otherwise have been. However, I do know that if we do not start doing something to reach fatherless young men in our culture, the prison rates and incidence of men abandoning their families will continue to escalate from generation to generation.

For moms, with their protective nature, it can be difficult to watch their son be stretched and tested by an older man (whether related or not). But for most boys, these are exactly the kind of challenges they need to overcome in order to develop a healthy masculinity.

We are not talking about brutalizing a boy here, but we are talking about pushing him so that he learns his worth and value. Males gain self-esteem through their accomplishments. Because women gain self-esteem through relationships, they often fail to understand this key component to a male's development. A woman can *tell* a boy all day long that he is special, but let a man push a boy to accomplish a difficult task and he will truly believe he is special.

The gift of resiliency allows boys to build their own character by following through on tasks when they get tough. It builds healthy self-esteem in a male when he is able to withstand the difficulties of life.

Perseverance

All men who have achieved significance had one trait in common—they all persevered through the difficulties of life. Abolitionist William Wilberforce spent his entire life fighting an uphill battle against slavery in England, being attacked and criticized continuously, only learning he had succeeded on his deathbed. Michael Jordan was cut from his high school basketball team before becoming the greatest basketball player who ever lived. Winston Churchill was the one man who never quit when most of his fellow countrymen were ready to throw in the towel against Nazi Germany, and consequently he nearly single-handedly saved his country from defeat. Abraham Lincoln is perhaps one of our greatest presidents and a man who faced the toughest times of our country's history. Looking at Lincoln's history gives us an opportunity to see how he developed these sterling qualities of manhood. Lincoln's mother died when he was nine years old and he was basically forced to educate himself. Lincoln failed in several business ventures; was defeated for legislative, congressional, and senate seats several times; and lost his sweetheart to illness, all before finally being elected president of the United States in 1860. He went on to lead this country during the time of the greatest loss of human life in our history, he abolished slavery, and he reconciled the country before his life was cut short by an assassin's bullet.

Lincoln admitted he failed a lot, but he never quit. In fact, he never considered himself a quitter or a failure. He learned from his losses and mistakes. His persistence in the face of great adversity contributed to his toughness, built his character, and hardened his will. He learned perseverance, humility, strength, determination, and wisdom from his failings. His failures prepared him to be uniquely qualified to lead an entire country gripped in the most desperate of circumstances at a time when it was being torn apart from within. That's the kind of men we need to produce today.

Never allowing our boys to fail—or rescuing them at the first sign of distress—prevents them from developing these important masculine core values. Falling and getting back up to try again and again prepares them to lead their families through even the toughest times without quitting.

One lesson we need to teach our boys is that to fail when attempting great things is not failure. Quitting is failure. Doing the right thing for the right reason and failing is not failure—it is faithfulness. And God always honors faithfulness.

Finally, learning to quit is a habit that males can easily develop. Boys who learn to quit grow up to be men who quit when things become difficult. Perhaps two of the most difficult things in life are being married and raising a family. Men who were trained as boys to quit or were always rescued when things got tough will be more apt to leave when relationships are difficult. All relationships have difficult times. The nature of a relationship has ups and downs, peaks and valleys. The ability to weather the valleys makes the peaks much more enjoyable. Those who quit fail to receive the joy of those high peaks. It is part of the reason our divorce rate is so high. People fail to find the joys in marriage because they do not persevere through the difficult times.

Integrity

> Some men see things as they are and say why. I dream things that never were and say why not.
>
> Robert F. Kennedy

Many people identify integrity as one of the best characteristics a man can have, but they do not know what integrity actually means. If asked, most people will say it means honesty or character. Those traits are part of what make up having integrity, but having integrity is actually more of a lifestyle or code that permeates a man's life than it is any specific character trait. The *Merriam-Webster Collegiate Dictionary* defines integrity as:

1. firm adherence to a code of especially moral or artistic values : INCORRUPTIBILITY 2. an unimpaired condition

: SOUNDNESS 3. the quality or state of being complete or
undivided : COMPLETENESS

I really like the first definition—incorruptibility (although soundness and completeness are also pieces of the
pie). The dictionary defines *incorruptibility* as "incapable
of corruption; not subject to decay or dissolution, incapable of being bribed or morally corrupted."

If we could raise sons to have integrity as defined above,
we would truly have raised men who would change the
world, don't you think?

Unfortunately, it seems to be the rule and not the excep-
tion today that people justify using whatever means necessary in order to achieve their goals. Athletes in nearly every
sport are routinely caught cheating by using performance-
enhancing drugs. Fans of those players readily forgive
them and even welcome them back from whatever minor
consequence they are forced to endure. One star baseball
player was recently suspended for fifty games for testing
positive for steroids and was hailed as a conquering hero
by fans and players upon his return. Corporate CEOs are
arrested for stealing employees' retirement funds, then
given minor sentences in country-club prisons and fined
a fraction of the money they embezzled. Movie stars and
musicians are frequently arrested for drug use and are
repeatedly sent to rehab with no other consequences for
their behavior. These supposed role models and leaders
may be marginally repentant because they got caught,
but the message to young people is "the ends justify the
means." The other message is that if you have enough
fame or money, the rules do not apply to you.

So how does a young man develop integrity? Integrity
is developed first and foremost by a boy or man making
an internal commitment. We then also help boys learn to

have integrity by teaching them self-discipline through being held accountable for their actions, decisions, and choices. Boys also need to learn that integrity has a cost associated with it. Frequently we do the right thing for the right reasons and do not get good results. It does not mean that we quit doing the right thing. Additionally, young men need to learn early that every decision or choice they make (or don't make) in life has a consequence associated with it. It's not always fair, but it's always true.

Men and boys with integrity live by a code. They don't waver in their convictions and are not swayed by peer pressure. They do not fold under the pressure of criticism. They are loyal and cannot be corrupted. They know what values they believe in and stay true to them throughout their lives. Men of integrity bless the lives of those who brush against them.

Respect

> Try not to become a man of success but rather try to become a man of value.
>
> Albert Einstein

Perhaps I'm just a curmudgeonly old guy now, but it seems to me that people are just not as respectful as they used to be. Much of our culture believes that you do not have any obligation to respect someone unless or until they respect you first. It is a twisted vision of biblical respect. First Peter 2:17 says, "Show proper respect to everyone." It doesn't say show proper respect if and only if they respect you in the way you think you deserve to be respected. It says to respect everyone because everyone was created in the image of God.

Maybe I'm the only one outraged and deeply disturbed by this downward shift in our cultural value system. But it does seem that young people are less respectful than my generation was. They seem to have a perverted concept of what constitutes respect. Many young men today believe they should be respected before they will offer respect. The fallacy in this philosophy is that respect is earned, not bestowed. When I was young, I would not have even considered being disrespectful to an adult, especially one in a position of authority. Additionally, if I had gotten in trouble in school, I would have suffered not only disciplinary actions from the school, but I would have been punished twice as bad when I got home. I can tell you from talking to and working with teachers, coaches, police officers, and parents that our children are for the most part very disrespectful toward any kind of authority.

This disrespect for authority (parents, teachers, police) creates a lack of integrity because they have no accountability in their lives. Young men without accountability have no need to be dependable, honest, or trustworthy in their words or actions. Why should they? No one else seems to care.

The lack of civil discourse in our culture also disturbs me. People on both sides of any issue resort to name-calling and out-shouting each other rather than intelligently and concisely stating their opinions and respectfully discussing them. Shouting down our opponents blinds our eyes to the validity of their points or truth that is being spoken. It makes the issue one of emotions instead of critical thinking. Anyone who doesn't share your opinion is ignorant and morally corrupt (racist, bigoted, judgmental). The belief that someone who has a different opinion than you do makes them somehow ignorant or less intelligent is not true.

This strategy of viciously attacking anyone who disagrees with you rather than politely listening and acknowledging their point of view before debating its merits is troubling for several reasons. First, it teaches young people that whoever is first to discredit and besmirch someone who disagrees with them is in the right. Of course political correctness and relativism promote that there are no rights or wrongs—except if you disagree with the prevailing belief system in power. In fact, there have been many high-profile examples where the truth has been spoken or written about, and because it somehow offended someone's *perceived* sensibilities, the author was attacked and marginalized to the point that the truthfulness of the statement ceased to be the issue and the political correctness of the topic overruled it. Those who promote tolerance the loudest are generally those who are actually the most intolerant of anyone who does not believe what they believe in. This mentality wants to edit and remove legitimate words from the English language because they are somehow "offensive."

Our young people are not being taught critical-thinking skills but are instead being taught to automatically judge and despise anything that our culture says is somehow offensive—like absolute truth. In reality they are being manipulated through their emotions instead of using principles and common sense as guidelines to discover the truth. Judging by the percentage of songs and movies now that are remakes of older ones, I think even the creativity of our young people has been stifled by this kind of political correctness—no one thinks outside the box or beyond what is culturally acceptable and so no new ideas are developed. Political correctness is stifling the creativity of our culture.

Next, this mentality stops the normal discussion process necessary to capitalize on the ideas and intellect of people from all sides of an issue. It also stops a majority of people from expressing their opinion for fear of attack. I have friends who would make incredibly good politicians and would change our country for the better. But they refuse to run for office because they know their value system will cause them to be subject to unrelated attacks on their character, which will at best render them ineffective and at worst destroy their reputation and even their lives.

Lastly, this kind of behavior is dishonorable. It teaches people to show contempt for and ridicule those who are different than they are instead of honoring them for their positive faculties. (I imagine people on the right and the left are thinking I am talking about the other side right now, but in fact I am talking about both of you—you are both guilty and should be ashamed of yourselves.)

When we act the way described above, are we conducting ourselves with honor and giving honor to others? Does out-shouting each other exhibit honesty, fairness, integrity, and high respect? And more to the point—if children are raised under those cultural expectations, will they be more likely to use that strategy with their spouse and children when disagreements occur? I'm just saying . . .

Honor

Any nation that does not honor its heroes will not long endure.

Abraham Lincoln

Honor is defined on Dictionary.com as having three facets: (1) honesty, fairness, and integrity; (2) a source of credit or distinction; or (3) high respect.

Honor and honor codes are extremely important to boys and men. Throughout history the one common element of masculine culture in every civilization appears to be the presence of some sort of honor code among men. Most of these honor codes were noble in nature. Warrior codes are often infused with honor: the medieval knights with their code of chivalry, Samurai of feudal Japan with their death-before-dishonor code, and even our country's US Marines motto of *Semper Fidelis* (always faithful) all have or had clear rules a man lived his life by. These honor codes held men to a set of ideals and principles that enabled them to live a more noble life. Typically the willingness to sacrifice the self for the greater good is seen as the most important defining characteristic of a man of honor or a hero.

Men need to believe in something worth dying for. They need a code to live by that holds them to a higher standard than they are capable of by themselves. To belong to a cause or quest greater than themselves makes them feel noble. Men will gladly sacrifice their lives if they have an honor code to live by, if they have some truths worthy of sacrifice. But men who do not have an honor code to live by often behave erratically. One only need look at the abhorrent behavior of predominantly fatherless boys and young men who join gangs in urban inner-city areas. These young men make their own honor codes that are destructive to themselves and to others.

Unfortunately, our current culture of relativism has left us with no real truths (everything being relative) and thus nothing is worth dying for. This teaches young men that nothing is honorable or noble. Cynicism and apathy rule the day. The concept of honor appears to have declined in importance in the modern secular Western culture, but young males still yearn for it.

After being discharged from the military in the late 1970s, I started working for a large, popular nightclub. I designed and operated the lighting and sound systems for the bands and nationally known entertainers who played at the club. My other responsibility between sets was to act as a backup for the doorman and bouncer, a big guy named Kelly. From the first day of work, Kelly and I immediately felt a connection and quickly became best friends. We began an intense workout regimen together where we spent most of our days lifting weights and running across tough terrain before working nights. After work we often played just as hard as we worked out. Being handsome, healthy, well-developed young men in the full prime of our masculinity, we never lacked for opportunity.

Since both Kelly and I came from homes without positive male role models (Kelly's dad died early in life and I was raised in an alcoholic home), we were both unconsciously interested in a masculine honor code. In retrospect, while we didn't express it this way, I think we were both searching for guidelines to give our lives meaning and significance. Somehow, we stumbled upon referring to ourselves as "The Monsieurs" (pronounced "monsewers"). This nomenclature soon took on its own persona as we steadily defined how Monsieurs behaved and what they could and couldn't do. It was a self-imposed honor code that combined a somewhat warped sense of chivalry with our idea of refined behavior. For instance, a Monsieur never dallied with a married woman, he maintained high standards of personal appearance and grooming, he never cheated or lied, and he always protected women and children and those who couldn't defend themselves. We once (after an early morning power workout) came around a corner in downtown Portland to find a couple of teenage boys surrounded by an urban gang. As the Monsieurs suddenly showed up and confronted the situation with wicked grins on their faces, the gang members decided to sullenly disperse and slink away. It was like a scene from an old West showdown.

As the reputation of the Monsieurs grew, others began referring to us in the third person. In fact, we even had a number of groupies who routinely came to the club just to hang around the Monsieurs. It wasn't that we took ourselves seriously, but I think we were just eager to have some sort of honor code to live by—something that defined us, set us apart, and gave us a higher standard to strive toward.

The legend of the Monsieurs lives on to this day (at least in our minds). Kelly and I and our wives occasionally get together for dinner and rehash old stories of our glory days. And my son has grown up with the legend of the Monsieurs and wants to be a "Garçon," sort of an honorary, young Monsieur. He too strives for something that defines him and identifies him with greatness or at least imposes upon him a higher standard to live by.

Without honor, a man's life is shallow and empty of purpose. An honor code gives males guidelines to follow and guardrails to protect them from running off the path of life. Without these "rules of life," a man is left to weigh individual decisions on a case by case basis. This means that men will be more likely to compromise during times of struggle than they will during times of plenty.

Temptations seldom occur when we are best prepared to resist them. They have a way of sneaking up on us and attacking unexpectedly. We need to seriously think about these kinds of moral and ethical choices before we are faced with them. Having an established code of honor in place with people who hold us accountable to that code keeps us boys and men from making choices we will regret later. When we have a "line in the sand" that we know we won't cross, it means we don't have to have any moral ambiguity about the choices we are faced with. Having a code of honor keeps us from using situational ethics or being influenced by our emotions instead of a set of principles. Men who fall into one of those two traps make decisions they wish had never been made. Those decisions end up hurting not just them but other people as well.

Questions for Reflection and Discussion

1. What is more important to our sons: what we say or what we do?

2. Are parents more influential than cultural icons in teaching their children (even teenagers) a value system?

3. What character traits do you think are important for a man to have? Have you started a proactive plan to teach your son those traits?

4. Why is integrity important in the lives of males? What effects does a lack of integrity cause within a culture?

5. Do you think honor is important to males? Why or why not?

11

SELF-DISCIPLINE

Train Him Up in the Way . . .

*There was a time when we expected nothing of children
but obedience, as opposed to the present, when we expect
everything of them but obedience.*

Anatole Broyard

THERE'S AN OLD saying that talks about "picking your
battles, not your nose." This means you have to be
careful to choose only those battles that matter in the
big picture or you will lose the war. It also means that by
doing nothing, you lose. This is a good strategy when raising teenage boys. One of the battles you should choose is
teaching him self-discipline. Self-discipline might be the
key to mastering noble character. Aubrey Andelin says,
"Males are inclined to be carnal, sensual, lazy, irrespon-

sible, selfish, and filled with fear."[1] The key to overcoming these weaknesses is through self-discipline.

I'm inclined to believe that males need strict boundaries and high expectations placed upon them in order to be successful. Boys learn best by trial and error, through experiences. It is generally always best to allow them to suffer the consequences of their choices. Because of their nurturing nature, many moms want to rescue their sons from anything unpleasant. But, as we've discussed earlier, boys who are rescued too often seldom lead successful lives. The following are a few areas in which it might be important to allow your son to grow, even if it means learning from the "hard knocks" of life.

Boundaries

This past season, several high-profile college head football and basketball coaches have been vilified and lost their jobs due to the perception that they harshly enforced disciplinary methods upon a player or players in their program. I'm not defending these coaches' methods, as I do not know the situation, but here's what I do know. Many young men today, especially talented athletes, have been raised without a father or any other accountability or boundaries in their lives. They have gotten whatever they want their entire lives. They do not understand the value of true leadership or the concept of respect. These young men rebel against any kind of discipline and despise authority figures. Even though they may in truth crave discipline, they have steered their own ship for too long. They have learned to do what they want when they want, and so any kind of restrictions—whether it is healthy for them or not—are very uncomfortable. They instinctively

Steps to Self-Mastery

Author Aubrey Andelin states that self-mastery (self-discipline) is gained through three steps: training the will, prayer, and fasting. Here are some steps your son can take to train his will:

1. Do something you don't want to do and do it regularly—do an unpleasant job you have been procrastinating, take a cold shower, take out the trash, perform other chores without being asked.
2. Deprive yourself of something pleasant—decide not to watch your favorite TV show, give up snacks or desserts, break a bad habit.
3. Demand defined quotas of yourself—rise early each morning to finish a goal you set, exercise each day, read a book every day.
4. Do something difficult—set goals that are difficult but not impossible and finish to completion.[2]

resist accountability and become self-focused and self-absorbed. Without willingly acceding to the mentorship and authority of other men, young males with this attitude will struggle their entire lives, creating problems in the lives of those who love and depend upon them.

Teaching boys self-discipline is difficult and requires effort on your part. Like most things worthwhile in life, it is hard. Boys learn best by what is modeled *for* them, not spoken *to* them. Teaching them self-discipline requires that *you* be disciplined. Constantly indulging your son in his every desire isn't good for him. It doesn't mean you have to be harsh or mean, but you do have to say no sometimes, even frequently. For moms who feel guilty about the circumstances in which they are raising their sons, this can be difficult. For some parents today, pushing their sons to teach them self-discipline almost feels like child abuse. But the truth is that the more you can teach them to have a strong sense of self-discipline, the happier and healthier they will be throughout their entire lives.

Most parents pull away from teenagers, assuming they need more space and freedom. Actually, they need you more than ever. Stick with them. If you don't, they will assume you don't care and wonder why you left them on their own. Boys especially need strong boundaries. They are more comfortable knowing what the rules are and what is expected of them.

Boundaries are a must during the teenage years. Boundaries help instill self-discipline. Without boundaries boys do not know what the rules are and what is expected of them. They may rebel, but remember that no matter what they say, the very fact that you thoughtfully and consistently enforce rules of behavior makes them feel loved and valued. They might complain to their friends that you are mean and tough, but they will say it with a sense of pride too. I've known many at-risk young men who have told me that they wished their parents had loved them enough to make them follow a set of guidelines designed to keep them safe.

Recognize though that boundaries need to be flexible to grow and change as your son does. Just like your son is constantly growing and changing, so too his boundaries should be dynamic. To hold a seventeen-year-old young man to the same boundaries he had as a thirteen-year-old boy would certainly cause rebellion at best and psychological damage at worst. As he shows more maturity and responsibility, his boundaries should be loosened to help him continue to grow in his decision-making and critical-thinking skills process. Our goal is to help him become a healthy, functioning adult by the time he is out from under our umbrella. By not allowing him to grow, we are doing him a disservice by ensuring his failure in the world.

That said, all children (even teens) need clear-cut rules, structure, and guidelines in order to develop self-discipline. They thrive under firm supervision and guidance—they need strong boundaries and discipline from adults. They don't need you to be their friend. They have plenty of friends. They need you to teach them the things they will need to be successful in life. And sometimes that requires courage on your part. Teens (especially strong-willed ones) know how to push buttons—they are developing their critical-thinking skills so they like to argue. They are masters at manipulation. They wear you down—it's part of their battle strategy. That's one reason it is important for a husband and wife to be on the same team. They must work together to ensure that a child is raised with consistency and with the same agenda. The bane of many divorced families is that Mom and Dad have a differing value system in their respective homes. Kids are confused from week to week as to what is expected of them.

Discipline comes in two forms—internal and external. Internal discipline or self-discipline is what we strive to teach our kids by applying external discipline. External discipline is applied in a variety of forms—suffering the consequences of their actions, experiencing the pleasures of delayed gratification, understanding the relationship between hard work and success, and being personally accountable. Kids who are not subjected to healthy discipline while growing up tend to live unhappy lives and create chaos in the lives of those around them. When we discipline our kids, we are actually preparing them for much more fulfilling lives.

Think of it this way. Self-discipline is a gift you give your son that will benefit him his entire life. It will benefit your grandchildren and your great-grandchildren as well.

Like all things that are important in life, though, learning self-discipline is difficult and requires hard work. One of the most effective ways to teach a boy self-discipline is by holding him accountable for his actions and choices. The sooner he learns that every decision he makes (or doesn't make) has consequences associated with it, the sooner he starts making disciplined and healthy choices. This will be extremely important when he becomes a man and his choices have magnified consequences to both him and his family. Want to see this in action? The next time your son wants an item from the store, tell him, "Sure, you can have it if you buy it with your own money." You'll quickly see what he places value on when he has to be responsible for purchasing it himself.

Managing Chores

I am convinced more than ever of the importance of boys having to do chores from a young age. Whether or not they earn an allowance for the chores they do, they should still contribute to the operation of the household as part of a team. Given the option, boys will generally choose not to do anything around the house. Allowing them to not participate in chores teaches them to be slovenly, lazy, and disobedient. It encourages a lack of self-discipline. Having tasks to perform on a consistent basis establishes habits that last a lifetime. It helps boys become self-reliant and responsible. Therefore they must be made to fulfill their responsibilities. This should be a nonnegotiable part of his upbringing.

As we discussed elsewhere in this book, males garner much of their self-esteem and self-image from their success and performance at their jobs. A boy who does not learn how to work and successfully accomplish tasks that are assigned to him has a greater struggle being successful in the workplace. Since he will work for most of his life, the sooner he learns to enjoy it, the better off he will be.

However, I think it is important that a boy does get an allowance if at all possible. Having an allowance gives parents the opportunity to teach a young man valuable lessons on how to manage money and stay out of debt. While it is important that he do things around the house as part of his contribution to the family, having the opportunity to earn an allowance is valuable as well. This provides the opportunity to teach him many valuable life lessons, including saving for an important purchase (delayed gratification) or saving for a rainy day, tithing (donating), budgeting his finances, and knowing the difference between needs and wants. Not only that, but it gives him a realistic perspective on the value of things. If he has to work in order to earn the money to purchase something, it means more to him and he will appreciate it more and take better care of it. You can see this in smaller, less expensive items, but the area I noticed it the most in was the purchase of a car. We purchased one of our children's first automobile for them, and frankly they didn't take very good care of it. The second child had to purchase one from money they had earned, and it was amazing how much more they appreciated it and kept it well maintained.

Additionally, encourage your son, even as a young teen, to find opportunities to earn money on his own. I had a lawn mowing business and a newspaper route when I was twelve years old and was able to purchase almost all of my school clothes from then on. After your son turns sixteen years old, insist that he get a part-time job. My friends and I worked in hamburger joints or gas stations when we were in high school. This not only teaches him the value of money but also helps prepare him for life after he leaves your home. During high school, our son was involved in orchestra, jazz band, student leadership, several sports, and was attempting to earn his Eagle Scout badge. After that, he attended college for a year and was involved in the jazz band. We allowed our son to not work at a job during high school or college. We justified it by believing that the activities he was involved in were all worthwhile, and we did not want to take him away from those experiences. But in hindsight, it was difficult to force him to get a job after he stopped attending college. I now believe he would have been better off with fewer extracurricular activities and more work experience.

As your son becomes an older teen, I would also encourage you to gradually start turning over specific costs to him. For instance, some parents make their sons pay their own car insurance, cell phone bills, clothing costs, and car payment. Certainly after he is out of school he should pay rent if he still lives in your home. This prepares him for what he will encounter in the real world after having been sheltered by your care.

Managing Money—Credit Card Debt

Perhaps the biggest problem most of us face in the United States is being good financial stewards. Debt is a significant problem for most families, and the biggest reason for marriage breakups is reported to be stress from finances. Up to 2.5 million people seek credit counseling each year to avoid bankruptcy. The average person seeking help has $43,000 in credit card debt. There were 173 million credit card holders in the US in 2006, with that number expected to rise to 181 million by 2010. Total consumer debt in 2009 was $2.5 trillion.[3]

Nearly one-third of high school students have a credit card. But only one in three knows how to read a bank statement, balance a checkbook, and pay bills.[4] Nellie Mae reports that the average college student owes $2,700 in credit card debt. Almost eight out of ten college students have at least one credit card and 32 percent have at least four credit cards.[6]

Money Management Tips for College Students

1. Join a credit union.
2. Do not use a credit card.
3. Avoid nonacademic debt.
4. Save up and pay cash for all purchases.
5. Pay bills on time.
6. Spend less than you earn.[5]

Suffice it to say, having knowledge and experience in handling finances gives a young person a big advantage in life. Truthfully, because we did not understand credit debt and how it works, the first purchase my wife and I made as soon as we got married was a new car. We have been under the heavy burden of debt ever since.

One of the most amazing things in the world is the power of compound interest. As a high school graduation gift for each of our children, we purchased them a $500 IRA account. We wanted to give them something that would be of value longer than a watch, a television, or a trip to a beach somewhere. We also wanted them to learn about the power of compound interest. We encouraged them to have a minimal amount ($25) of money deducted each month from their paycheck and direct deposited into the account. If they are faithful in doing this, in twenty-five years they would have accumulated $37,871.88. In forty-five years (when they are sixty-three years old), they would have $273,684. If they were really serious and saved $100 per month over forty-five years, their initial deposit and the money they actually saved would be $54,500. But because of compound interest, the amount in their account would be worth nearly one million dollars ($985,400).

I wish someone would have explained to me the power of compound interest when I was a young person just starting out in life.

Managing Time

Most young men today struggle with juggling their time between job, school, friends, significant relationships, and sleep. In this context it is difficult for them to find time for meaningful activities like volunteering or even worship. Young men also report they find it difficult to find time for themselves.

I believe that learning to utilize your available time is what separates people who are successful in life from those who are not. Time is a finite and precious resource. Once gone, it cannot be regained. Yet I observe many people who waste large amounts of their time. As a businessman, I have always had the motto that time is money. That helped me put into perspective the value of my time so I didn't waste it. People frequently tell me they don't know how I can get so much accomplished in such a short period of time. My ability to efficiently use my time to its maximum potential allows me to accomplish more than many of my friends and peers. It even allows me to overcome shortcomings in areas where I am weak.

The few tips I've learned over the years are pretty simple yet quite effective. First of all, I am a big believer in lists. If something is not written down, it generally does not get done. So I make a list in the evening of everything I want or need to accomplish the next day. Even if it is something I know I have to do every day for a long period of time (like write a book), I still write it down every day so I know I have to work on it. Otherwise it tends to get pushed into the background as seemingly more important issues arise. I then try to do the more difficult or burdensome tasks first while I am fresh and have a lot of energy. Anything that I do not accomplish or finish completely that day goes on the list for the next day (if it is not moot by then).

As our children were growing up, every year on New Year's Eve we would have a big family dinner together and each of us would share a written "Goals List" for the coming year. Our encouragement for our children was that they would put this list in a place (like the bathroom mirror) where they would see it frequently throughout the year. We would also review our previous year's list to see what we had accomplished and what we did not—and why. The actions of writing down our dreams and desires and looking at them every day seemed to make them miraculously come true quite often. Perhaps the psychological prompting caused our subconscious to make decisions that worked toward attaining those goals.

Next, most people do not accomplish much because they are overwhelmed by the magnitude of a project and find themselves paralyzed into inaction. For instance, hundreds of people every year tell me they are going to write a book (just about everyone I meet says they are going to write a book). Well, only a miniscule amount of those people actually do write a book. Not because they can't but because it is difficult and takes a lot of hard work. It is such a big task they don't even know where to start—so they don't. I have found that if you want to do something, the most important thing you can do is just start doing it. You'll quickly learn what you need to know in order to accomplish it. If you wait for everything to be perfect before you start, you'll never start. This is where perseverance comes in. It's like the old question, "How do you eat an elephant?" The answer: "One bite at a time."

I can always tell where people place their priorities by how they spend their time. For example, someone might tell me they are too busy to go back to school and get their degree, yet I see them spending a lot of time playing video games. Obviously they do have the time to go to school; they just place a higher priority on playing video games. Personally I don't care how anyone spends their time. It just annoys me when people use how busy they are as an excuse for why they aren't accomplishing what they claim they want to in life.

If your son can learn the difference between wasting his time and the value of his time, he will be much further ahead than most people in the world. That doesn't mean that he cannot take time to enjoy himself, just that he is conscious of the fact that there are only twenty-four hours in each day and that those hours must be allocated properly to accomplish his goals in life.

Of course, that means that he must actually *have* goals in life. Many young men are directionless and drift aimlessly along without any goals or dreams. Then one day they wake up and wonder, "How in the heck did I get where I am?"

One of our main goals as parents is to prepare our children to go out into the world and live productive, successful, happy lives. People who utilize their time effectively tend to be much happier, productive, and successful.

Questions for Reflection and Discussion

1. Why is self-discipline important?

2. Give some examples of ways to teach young men self-discipline.

3. Does your son have chores that he is required to perform on a consistent basis?

4. Have you taught your son how to manage a budget yet? How about how a credit card works?

5. What are some ways to teach your son how to manage his most valuable commodity—time?

12

LEADERSHIP

Teaching Your Son to Be a Leader

Don't measure yourself by what you have accomplished,
but by what you should have accomplished with your
ability.

John Wooden

I THINK ALL MOMS want their sons to grow up to be leaders. They would like them to be strong leaders of their families, in their communities, and in their spiritual walk. I believe leaders are developed, not born. But teaching boys how to be leaders requires intentionality. Here are some factors to keep in mind as you develop a plan to train your boy to become a leader.

Setting High Standards

The expectations we have for our children tend to come to fruition. With that in mind, I think it is important we have high expectations for our boys. Why not exhort them to aspire to greatness? The rule of thumb in the business world is that employees are only capable at best of living up to about 75 percent of the expectations that an employer has for them. Why should we strive to produce mediocre men by having low expectations of our boys?

Unfortunately, our culture not only has low expectations for males, it seems to revel in trying to destroy masculinity. For the most part, young men in our culture have not been challenged beyond the expectation that they support themselves economically. We have no higher expectations of manhood. Paul Coughlin comments on what our culture does to boys: "Boys are being gunned down by manliness gone bad and by those who do not accept or appreciate it. Our culture tells young boys that traditional masculinity is bad, that men are stupid and deserve to be the object of disdain, contempt, and ridicule. Then we expect them to grow up and exemplify honor, integrity, and valor."[1] Just watch nearly any television sitcom or commercial if you doubt that statement.

True manhood accepts responsibility for others' lives by protecting, providing, nurturing, and leading those under its sphere of influence. But how do we teach boys the lessons they need in order to accept that responsibility and develop the mind-set necessary to fulfill those roles?

In many cultures throughout history, manhood was something that was earned through overcoming difficult challenges or dangerous initiations. It involved initiations, rituals, and ceremonies generally supervised by older males. Frequently the instructions passed along during these rites of passage contained life lessons that taught boys what it meant to fulfill the roles and responsibilities of manhood.

Teaching young men to have empathy and compassion for others is very important in the development of a healthy man. It has been my experience from raising two teenagers and working with many others that they are often idealistic about the world and troubled by the injustices that abound within it. The current version of a centuries-old quote says, "If you're not a liberal at twenty you have no heart, if you're not a conservative at forty you have no brain." Young men *should* be indignant and disturbed by things like poverty, victimization, and exploitation of those who cannot defend themselves. That outrage means they have heart. It is much better than the passive, apathetic, and self-focused attitude many young (and older) men possess today. Instead our culture tells them that self-gratification and self-indulgence are worthier goals.

Let's look at some of the factors we need to be aware of and some activities that teach the lessons boys need to learn.

Inspiring a Vision

Tony Rorie is the founder of a program called Men of Honor in Dallas, Texas. Men of Honor exists to make passionate followers of Christ by mentoring and training next generation leaders ages eleven to seventeen in the principles of chivalry, honor, integrity, moral excellence, and courageous leadership. They use a three-pronged strategy of life-changing camps, conferences, and curriculum. The camps are weekend encounters where youth go through rites of passage, leadership development exercises, and powerful encounters with the Holy Spirit. The most important Father's Blessing is imparted by older male mentors to mostly fatherless youth. Camp graduates are then connected to weekly curriculum-based mentoring groups where they are taken through Dr. Ed Cole's Majoring in Men curriculum and taught that manhood and Christ-likeness are synonymous. They believe that being a male is a matter of birth, but being a man is a matter of choice. Tony gave this powerful speech at a recent graduation:

> When this generation was born, there were three parties present: The Lord was there to name them according to their purpose. He named them Victorious Warrior, Mighty Deliverer, Faithful Servant, Overcomer, Light in the Darkness. Next their parent or, if they were fortunate, parents, named them: Dalton, Daniel, James, Lauren, Jordan. Then the enemy named them: Drug-Addict, Pornographer, Suicide Victim, AIDS Patient.
>
> This generation will fulfill two of those three names in their lifetime—which will it be? Thirty-six percent of this generation woke up this morning without their dad in the home. Whoever captures the heart of the next generation will name that generation. Modern marketers have begun their plans long ago. The enemy has begun his plans . . . to kill, steal, and destroy. These forces will spare no expense to see their plans come to reality.
>
> NEITHER WILL WE! We will spare no expense to see the plans of the Lord come to light in the hearts of young people. They are created in the image of God and bear His image. They are world changers, Kingdom builders—mighty servants of the Kings of Kings!
>
> Join us in our pursuit of this generation. Pray for Men of Honor as we establish life-changing opportunities for young people to hear the Good News of life through Jesus Christ, see their purpose and potential as world-changers, and stand up in their generation as leaders![2]

What a mighty, manly legacy to pass on to a group of boys entering manhood. All males, no matter their age, yearn for significance in their lives. They yearn for a battle to fight that means something. Young men run to the battlefield, not because they want to kill or be killed, but because they want to participate in a battle bigger than themselves—one that matters. They want the world to know they existed. God created them this way to make the world safe and healthy.

When we teach our sons the nobility of using the awesome masculine power that God gave them to help others, we give them the ability to define their lives—we channel that natural competitiveness, aggressive nature, and yearning for significance that God gave them into healthy, life-giving outlets. The world has many battles that need to be fought by a group of men and boys banding together. Things like poverty, child and domestic abuse, drug and alcohol abuse, illiteracy, sexual slavery and human trafficking, fatherlessness, and violent behavior. Just like men of yore were adventurers of wild continents, explorers of untamed lands, and conquerors of the unconquerable, we need to give our young men today adventures with noble causes to live their lives for. But without a vision to inspire them, many boys settle for a life lesser lived.

Passing the Mantle of Manhood (Rites of Passage)

Young men growing up without mentors are just boys seeking their identity. Since our culture does not have intentional rites of passage to teach and help guide young men from boyhood into manhood, they are often left to rely upon themselves to try to figure out how to become a man. Some boys consider getting drunk for the first time as the sign of crossing the threshold into manhood. Others think losing their virginity is surely a sign of being a man. At its extreme, gangs often require initiation ceremonies of new members that include assault and battery, theft, rape, or even murder. How hopeless and desperate does someone have to be that they would take the life of another human being for a sense of belonging?[3]

John Eldredge calls boys who have never been initiated and mentored into manhood "partial" men. They are boys walking around in men's bodies, sometimes even fulfilling their roles with jobs and families. For these men, the passing on of masculinity was never completed (if started at all). These boys were never taken through the process of masculine initiation. It's why many men today are what Eldredge calls "Unfinished Men."[4]

In his classic book *Raising a Modern-Day Knight*, Robert Lewis uses the model of initiating boys into manhood through the medieval custom of knighthood. In those times, boys were trained and equipped with a masculine vision, a code of conduct, and an objective to live life. First as a page, then as a squire, and finally as a knight, they passed through stages that trained them and helped instill in them a chivalric code of honor. At each of these stages they were given ceremonies that celebrated their achievement and marked their progress toward manhood. By the time they were ready to become knights, they had a clear definition of a man's duties and responsibilities and a code of conduct to live their life by. In other words, they knew what a man was because they had been trained and tutored by honorable men for many years. Perhaps the most important part of this process was when another man or men held a ceremony and bestowed the mantle of manhood upon them.

Lewis says this:

Ceremonies are those special occasions that weave the fabric of human existence. Weddings. Award banquets. Graduations. The day you became an Eagle Scout or were accepted into a fraternity. *We remember because of ceremony.* Think back upon the significant moments in your life. With few exceptions, the value of those moments was sealed by a ceremony. Someone took the time to plan the details, prepare the speech, and purchase the awards—so you would feel special. Ceremony should be one of the crown jewels for helping a boy become a man. In many cultures throughout history, a teenage boy is taken through some type of ritual to mark his official passage into manhood. I believe one of the great tragedies of Western culture today is the absence of this type of ceremony.[5]

Ceremonies or rites of passage are important for all children but especially for boys. Our children develop their faith not only from us but from others as well. Remember, someone is going to influence your children—it had better be you or at least those who have the same value system as you do.

While my son was growing up, a group of men along with our sons went through a modified program based on Robert Lewis's *Raising a Modern-Day Knight*. We based our program around the four A's: Acceptance (of each other), Affirmation (encouraging each other), Accountability (to one another), and Authority (under Christ). We adopted a "Knight's Code of Conduct" after studying Bible passages relating to servant leadership, self-discipline, kindness, perseverance, purity, integrity, humility, and loyalty. Each of the dads gave all the boys one of their business cards and encouraged them to contact any man at any time if they needed him. We would have a study one Saturday morning a month and then go to breakfast afterward.

Robert Lewis's Principles of Manhood

1. A Real Man Rejects Passivity: He rejects his natural inclination for social and spiritual passivity.
2. A Real Man Accepts Responsibility: He boldly accepts the responsibility for the well-being of his family and those who look up to him.
3. A Real Man Leads Courageously: He courageously leads with truth rather than surrender to his feelings.
4. A Real Man Expects the Greater Reward: He fulfills his roles joyfully because he recognizes the rewards it brings him.[6]

We also tried to all go on an outing (snow skiing, rafting, camping) once every quarter or so. Each of the six boys who went through that two-year program has turned out to be a pretty good young man.

I had also held several personal ceremonies with my son at various stages, such as at age twelve when I took him to dinner (food seems to be a big part of most of my ceremonies), gave him a purity ring, and talked about the challenges he was undertaking as he entered adolescence.

But when my son graduated from high school, I was determined to have a ceremony he would remember to launch him into the world. Several months beforehand, I contacted six godly men and asked them to pray about what God would have them share with a young man just starting out in life. Shortly after his graduation I rented a room in the back of a restaurant and hosted a dinner with my son and the six men. Each man took a turn in front of the others telling my son the mistakes he had made, his regrets, and the things he wished he could do over. They shared from their hearts the joys and sorrows of being a man, a father, and a husband. The men were powerfully vulnerable as they shared from the depths of their souls. I then got up and spoke to my son of the dreams I had for

226

his life and shared advice about life. I gave him my blessing as a father to a son and launched him into the world.

I videotaped the dinner for my son so he can watch it over and over. At the time, the event may have impacted the other men more than my son, but as my son gets older, this advice will be invaluable. I intend to have a similar ceremony before he gets married—gather a group of men who have been successfully married a long time to pass along their special insights on what it takes to be a husband and love a woman.

Our boys are blessed for a lifetime when we design and prepare ceremonies to mark their journey into manhood. These ceremonies tell them they are progressing along a road with the destination of manhood. They are mileposts that boys can use to track their progress and understand what is expected of them on the next portion of their journey. It eliminates confusion and the need to "prove" they're men—to themselves and others.

To become an effective leader, a boy has to be trained by many older men.

Developing Critical-Thinking Skills (Problem Solving)

Perhaps one of the most important things a person (especially a leader) can develop is the ability to think through an issue and discern the important aspects of that issue while not being distracted by the parts that are of no consequence. Your son needs to learn to distinguish between fact and opinion. He needs to understand how to compare and contrast information. Too often, important issues are clouded by emotions or hyperbole. In addition, with today's technology it is easy to establish something on the internet that quickly becomes assumed as fact. As an example, books, magazines, or newspapers printing "facts" that are not backed up by well-rounded research with cited sources are really just printing their opinion. Television news programs are notorious for this today.

If you want your son to be someone who is not easily swayed by political agendas, misinformation, or opinions, he needs to develop good critical-thinking skills.

How do you help a boy develop the critical-thinking skills that are crucial for him to learn in order to develop into a good problem solver? There are some basic ways to develop critical-thinking skills—but I encourage you to be creative and intentional in your approach. First, as difficult as it may be, allow your son to argue or debate issues that do not relate to emergency circumstances. He is developing the process of understanding how to look at an issue critically from different sides. You'll notice that sometimes, if you agree with him, he may even switch his opinion in the middle of an argument and argue the other side. Also, while it may be annoying, allow him to ask a lot of questions. That shows he has an active mind and is searching for information and knowledge (or else he's just being a pain, but you can hope for the former).

Encourage him to think logically. For some women, that may be a challenge. Use concrete examples whenever possible that lead to logical conclusions. For instance, someone may be able to effectively argue against the validity of gravity, but they will hit the ground if they jump off a building. Logic takes the emotion out of an argument. Also, allow him to think through an issue or problem—do not rush in and give him the answer right away. It takes the male brain longer than the female brain to process information.

Think out loud in front of him—that way he can see and hear how you puzzle through the process of solving a problem. Finally, challenge him to always look at both sides of an issue. If you get only one opinion of a subject, you cannot truly understand it. One of the great lessons I have learned in life is that you cannot understand another's pain if you have not walked in their shoes. This will serve him well later in life when he has a wife and children and issues are seldom simply black and white but are complicated shades of gray.

Training Up Leaders

> Pray not for lighter burdens, but for stronger backs.
> Theodore Roosevelt

As a culture we are losing our most valuable resource—male leadership. Young men have grown up in an age of cultural suspicion, and they have found that it is difficult to exercise any kind of leadership without raising someone's ire.[7]

Cultures that allow families and communities to exist with no stable, healthy male authority and leadership devolve into chaos. Healthy masculine leadership protects the weak. It uses its influence and power to provide safe, life-giving encouragement and provision.

A healthy man doesn't shirk his responsibilities. He undertakes tasks with a "can-do" attitude and does not gripe or grumble when they become difficult or times become tough. He provides for his family as part of his manly duty. He takes pride in solving his own problems. He willingly shoulders his duties and doesn't face his responsibilities sullenly. Aubrey Andelin says, "His acceptance of this responsibility adds substance to the faith his wife places in him when she leaves the security of her parents' home to make her way with him."[8]

Boys need to hear words like *strong, brave, talented,* and *noble* in order to assimilate their duty as leaders. They need to have the adults in their lives intentionally speak affirming language that inspires and uplifts them to willingly assume the mantle that leadership imposes upon them. They need to be taught to relish the satisfaction that duty and honor bring to a man.

I am blessed and fortunate to continuously see the fruits that my ministry labors produce. To live a life where people frequently contact you to say that you made a difference or changed their lives and the lives of their families is an awesomely gratifying experience that carries with it great responsibility. Many men who know me look at my life with envy, but few are willing to make the sacrifices or take the risks necessary to achieve it. We need to encourage boys from a young age that God has a special plan for their lives. We need to train them early to be leaders and prepare them for the responsibility that comes with that role. We need to be intentional in equipping them with a bigger vision of what life is about rather than just letting them "settle" for whatever life throws at them. We need to inspire them to use the gifts and powers that God has endowed them with to make a difference in the world.

When we do that, not only will men become men again, but the world will be better because of it.

Activities That Inspire Leadership

There are a number of activities we can encourage young males to participate in, in order to help develop healthy masculinity—activities that develop the powerful traits of compassion and leadership within males. Perhaps most important is to encourage a sense of helping others. Especially for teenagers (who tend to live in a world that revolves around themselves as the center of the universe), this takes the focus off them and places it on those less fortunate. To have the compassion and empathy to recognize their responsibility to someone other than themselves is an important trait for a man to discover.

So what kinds of activities propel males from boyhood into manhood, teaching them important traits such as strength, courage, perseverance, respect, compassion, and empathy? Are there certain experiences that mature a boy and help him learn the life lessons that he needs in order to become a healthy, productive man? There are. In fact, there are many—too many to discuss in one chapter. I am going to mention one that has been most notable in my life and so I can speak to it from experience. Other men have similar experiences with a variety of other activities. That is one of the reasons boys need a multitude of mentors in their lives. Just as all men are different, so too all boys relate to different circumstances.

With the keen insight into the human psyche that women and especially mothers possess, I encourage you to take this information and think about what experiences your son could benefit from in order to develop these fundamental traits so key to a man's success in life.

Sports

Football is like life—it requires perseverance, self-denial, hard work, sacrifice, dedication, and respect for authority.

Vince Lombardi

Many males (young and old) are attracted to sports for a variety of reasons. Sports provide a physical outlet to compete against other males in a healthy environment. Sports provide an outlet for the physical expression that males enjoy. Sports teach lessons such as respect for authority, self-discipline, teamwork, perseverance, and even compassion and respect for a worthy opponent. They are even a creative outlet for many males. Most of all, sports help develop leadership qualities in nearly all who participate.

Sports cross all racial and cultural differences by teaching boys equality—an important trait in a leader. It is hard to hate someone when you work hard side by side next to them and depend upon them to cover your back during the heat of competition. I played in a men's basketball league that contained men of all races, colors, ethnicities, and cultures, including blacks, whites, Hispanics, Muslims, Christians, and atheists. Cultural and religious differences were set aside and were secondary to the joy of fierce competition.

Natural competition is so crucial to male development that boys who play organized sports are less likely to do drugs, join gangs, and become antisocial than boys who do not.[9] Young adult males are enormously kinesthetic. Through sports they bond, feel the power of themselves, push their limits, learn about themselves as physical beings, and test their character. Sports provide a discipline for them. They bond with other men and test themselves through competitive sports. Most young men see sports as more than a physical outlet—it touches who they are.

Sports also have a clear set of unambiguous rules that everyone must follow. It levels the playing field and makes equals of everyone. It provides boundaries with firm consequences that everyone must follow. Boys know if they break a rule that a specific consequence will happen. There are no exceptions. Males thrive under this system. While moms sometimes think the consequences are unfair, boys know that rules are meant to be followed and they actually feel good about having some guidelines. What is fair for all is surely fair for one. This is one reason it is important when disciplining your son not to make threats if you are not prepared to carry them out. He thrives under healthy consequences but develops scorn for authority if allowed to get away with things he knows he shouldn't. Males need rules to live by.

Rules allow a male to adapt and develop parts of himself that help him compete and even excel against more gifted players. For instance, I know many players who are not as physically gifted as their counterparts, and yet because they outthink, outhustle, or outplay them, they make themselves into the better player. This teaches boys that there is more than one way to solve a problem. Just because you may not be gifted in one specific area does not mean you stop trying. You compensate by developing other facets of your personality and skill set. Boys who do not learn this ability will quit or never try many things in life because they fear the humiliation of failing and being considered inadequate. But to overcome a significant disadvantage through grit, perseverance, guile, and hard work provides a joy and self-confidence that lasts a lifetime. It is a hugely powerful life lesson for a boy to learn.

Sports also encourage your son to set challenging goals for himself in life. Sports push a boy to accomplish more than he thinks he is capable of. It is important for your son to recognize the importance of developing the self-discipline to push himself throughout life. Too many males seek the easy way through life, much to their detriment. Aubrey Andelin describes their loss this way: "As a man accepts challenging goals . . . he brings to himself opportunities to enhance his masculinity. In seeking the *easy road* and avoiding responsibility he denies himself opportunities for personal development. *The pursuit of easy things makes men weak*, whereas the pursuit of challenging goals, great responsibility, and difficult paths strengthen a man. . . . Generally there is a point of compromise at which parents, friends or family members will be satisfied, but the nobler self within will not be. To feel good about ourselves we must do our best."[10]

Additionally, sports teach valuable lessons about winning and losing. To win gracefully develops respect and empathy for his opponent. A man who wins poorly is scorned by his peers. To lose with dignity develops healthy humility so vital to a man's character. To lose and get back up to try again is a very valuable lesson to have in life. This lesson of perseverance helps males succeed at life and in relationships. It keeps marriages together and helps men get through other difficult circumstances in life, of which there are many.

A word of caution here: if your son is an athlete, you must take time to know what your son is putting into his body. It is trendy today for even young athletes to take performance-enhancing drugs such as steroids, human growth hormones, or other lesser known (and nonregulated) supplements in order to gain either a competitive edge or stay even with other athletes.

Anabolic steroids are artificially produced hormones similar to male testosterone. There are over 100 variations of anabolic steroids, all of which are illegal except with a prescription by a physician. Anabolic steroids stimulate

Risks of Anabolic Steroid Use in Males

- Testicular shrinkage
- Pain when urinating
- Breast development
- Impotency
- Sterility
- Baldness
- Increased risk for prostate cancer
- Stunted growth in adolescents[11]

muscle tissue growth by mimicking the effects of naturally produced hormones. They improve strength, endurance, and muscle mass. Serious and long-lasting effects of performance-enhancing drugs like anabolic steroids include health risks such as cancer, heart disease, stroke, and liver problems. Other side effects include premature hair loss or balding, mood swings (including anger, depression, and aggression), paranoia (including mania, psychosis, or suicide), high blood pressure, trembling, joint ache, and shortening of height.[12]

Even legal, over-the-counter supplements may contain chemicals that have unknown effects on the human body. New technology is constantly giving us information on the side effects of these products. Unfortunately, the technology to test these products lags behind the production and marketing of new ones.

I have lifted weights and played sports for most of my life. The only substances I have ever taken are natural protein shakes (without supplements) to help naturally produce muscle mass and recover from workouts sooner. I have also coached middle school and high school athletes for years. I am not a doctor or a nutrition expert, but it is my "unprofessional" opinion that if a high school athlete does not have health issues, he does not need to ingest anything beyond a well-balanced, healthy diet containing all the nutrients recommended by the Recommended Dietary Allowances (RDAs), the United States Recommended Daily Allowances (USRDAs), and the dietary recommendations of Diet and Health (Committee on Diet and Health, 1989). However, specific sports may require modifications of nutrient intake to meet the physiologic demands of that sport, but this should never include performance-enhancing drugs or supplements.

Take it upon yourself to investigate any products your son wants to ingest. Do not take your son's word that it is okay. Do not even accept his coach's permission or recommendation on a product without checking with your physician or other health care professional first. My experience has been that while there are some very good and knowledgeable coaches, most high school coaches are just teachers trying to pick up some additional income—they know less than many parents. And even though most parents of high school athletes think their children are good enough to receive a college scholarship, only a small percentage actually do. In addition, only a miniscule number of college athletes make the ranks of professional athletes. Your son's long-term health is too important to risk for some short-term gain that probably will not do anything to benefit him in the long run.

Sports is just one of many experiences that your son can use to help develop some of the internal character traits he needs in order to lay a foundation to become a healthy man and leader. I realize that many boys are not athletically inclined. My son benefitted greatly from being involved in activities such as band, school government, and Boy Scouts. Other activities might include chess club, school newspaper, choir, art, or drama, all of which can help a young man become a leader in life. Those activities and many others (the choices are only limited by your imagination) can teach him skills such as accountability, respect for authority, and the value of hard work, perseverance, and teamwork—important traits for leaders to recognize and understand. These types of activities provide opportunities for your son to develop his own leadership skills.

Understanding the traits that contribute to leadership, combined with teaching him a few foundational lessons that are important to a man's soul, will help him leap the chasm from boyhood to manhood—something that many men never accomplish.

Questions for Reflection and Discussion

1. How can you help your son to be an effective leader in life?

2. Why are the expectations we place on our sons important?

3. Why are "rites of passage" important to a young man's life? How can you help develop some ceremonies to mark his passage from childhood to manhood?

4. Why is male leadership important?

13

THINGS YOUR SON NEEDS TO KNOW TO COURT MY DAUGHTER

Miles Standish was cutting off men's ears for courting a girl without her parents' consent.

Henry Woodfin Grady

A S MY DAUGHTER nears the age of matrimony, I have been spending greater amounts of time pondering what type of young man I would give my blessing for her to wed (not that I probably have much choice in the matter). Besides the character traits outlined in chapter 10, there are a number of qualities that a young man should develop to succeed and live an exemplary life. I looked at these as nonnegotiable traits that a young man needed to

238

have before dating my daughter when she was a teenager. Now I am wrestling with what kinds of traits I want in the man who marries my daughter.

Here are my traits of the "perfect" man for her. I want a young man for my daughter who is confident and believes in himself but is not cocky; polite but not to the point of being obsequious; loving, kind, and compassionate but not feminized; intelligent but not a know-it-all; passionate about important issues but not a wacko; has a plan in life but is not obsessed; works hard but puts family first; is a leader but not overbearing; handsome but not pretty; and has potential and the desire to continue to learn and grow.

I want to look at the young man and automatically think to myself, *I like the cut of his jib*. Perhaps that's an unrealistic expectation, or maybe those traits are how I unconsciously desire to perceive myself.

As a man and a dad of a daughter, I am familiar with all the male codes of conduct and unwritten rules regarding women. Hence it is my duty to protect my daughter as best as possible. I did this in several ways when she was in high school. Since first impressions are important, I always wanted to leave a lasting memory during the first meeting with her suitors. Besides cleaning my handgun, scowling at them, and crushing their hand during the greeting, I also instituted the infamous "have lunch with Dad" policy. I believe this policy became well known around the high school during the years my daughter attended. If a boy looked like he was going to be sniffing around for more than a date or two, my daughter would casually tell him that one of the requirements to date her was that he had to call me and schedule a lunch date. That in and of itself ran off many weak-willed young men or ne'er-do-wells. This luncheon gave me the opportunity to assess the young

239

man's character, find out facts about his background (so I could track him down if I had to), and also instill some rules regarding dating my daughter.

While not all the guys that came around the house to date her (or slunk around in the background) exhibited some or all of the following traits, I always had an ideal in mind of the kind of man I wanted for her. My daughter is now a young adult not living under my roof, but hopefully she will adhere to these guidelines as well when she considers marrying a young man.

At the request of a number of moms of teenage sons I've heard from, I am committing to write out my list of traits that I think are important in a young man to be acceptable to see my daughter. I think most dads (and moms) would agree with me.

Work Ethic

One of the real disservices we do to our boys is to not teach them the value of hard work. I believe that part of a male's identity is created from the very act of work and (healthy or not) from the type of occupation he holds.

Many of the problems parents experience with their teenage sons can be solved through work. Give your son chores, make him get a part-time job, and keep him physically active. You'll have fewer problems with his attitude, with getting into trouble, and with sex if you can keep him mentally and physically tired. The military discovered many years ago that they could eliminate fighting, horseplay, and sexual preoccupation in boot camp by keeping hundreds of teenage young men so exhausted that they fell asleep as soon as their heads hit the pillow in the barracks at night.

Boys develop confidence and competency (which define their self-esteem) by accomplishing masculine chores that increase their skills and abilities. They learn this best under the guidance of a father or other older male. Masculine chores include activities like building things, yard work, pouring cement, repairing a car, fixing a home, painting a house, repairing a roof, plumbing, or any number of other things that are best accomplished by his own two hands, his muscular physique, and the sweat of his brow. Through physical work he builds his body, hardening his muscles, and increases his physical strength and endurance. Teddy Roosevelt was a sickly, weak boy who built himself into a man of impressive physique and unparalleled accomplishment through hard work and self-discipline.

Too many parents today (especially mothers) parent out of guilt. They allow their desire to make their children happy override their intuition and common sense. Parenting is not about making your children happy. It's about helping them grow strong and preparing them for successful life as an adult. Giving in and allowing them to satisfy their every whim only serves to give them a distorted view of life. Life isn't fair and it doesn't care about your child. The sooner your son learns that lesson, the more easily he can adjust his attitude to deal with that fact.

Our young adult son, Frank (twenty-three years old at the time of this writing), appears to have a fairly well-developed work ethic. He works both a full-time and a part-time job and gladly fulfills the requirements to maintain steady employment. But he readily, even eagerly, admits his aversion to any activity that requires him to sweat. Because of that, he is missing out on the joy and satisfaction that comes from the creative process of building

241

something from nothing with his own two hands. He is depriving himself of the self-esteem a man feels from tackling a project on his own and through his own initiative, ingenuity, and hard work accomplishing a task through the sweat of his brow.

Males are physical beings. We process information more easily when we move, we develop self-esteem through accomplishments, and we channel aggression into healthy physical activities. Without the chores and hard work that used to be necessary in order to survive, young males are turning more toward sedentary activities that keep them from becoming powerful physically, which in turn also diminishes their emotional and mental health.

Teach your son to work and everyone will be happier.

Compassion

> Nearly all men can stand adversity, but if you want to test a man's character, give him power.
>
> Abraham Lincoln

One of the older teen boys who attended this past year's Single Mom's Family Camp came from an extremely abusive background. Because of that, when he first arrived at camp, he was continually picking on younger kids and acting out in a destructive manner. The next morning he was taken fishing by the mentors of his group. He was very reluctant to fish at first and wanted to release the fish when he did catch one. He could not bring himself to gut and clean the fish no matter how it was explained that it was against the camp rules to release them and that you always eat what you catch. One of the mentors was finally able to get out of him why. He said, "I just can't kill that innocent fish—he hasn't done anything wrong and deserves to live!" This was perhaps a reflection of his inner thoughts regarding his own life experiences. The smallest boy in the group was subsequently given the task of cleaning the fish, which he was able to do with relish (this served to elevate his status within the group). For the rest of the camp, the older boy's behavior was reflective; he was nicer to others and appeared calmer and gentler. This experience awakened within him a compassion that he might not have tapped into without it.

Surprisingly, another activity that is very healthy in the emotional development of boys is hunting. Societal wisdom might suggest that killing an animal (hunting) breeds violence and cruelty in males. But research suggests just the opposite is true. Hunting actually develops respect and reverence for life and other universal virtues in males such as generosity, fortitude, respect, patience, humility, and courage.

According to noted family therapist and bestselling author Michael Gurian, hunting paradoxically makes males more empathetic and develops responsibility, fairness, and compassion. Besides war, it is the most powerful way for males to learn these virtues. Gurian contends that healthy, safe hunting under the guidance and training of mentors actually produces a holistic experience that creates less violence in young males. In contrast, the one-dimensional experience of violent video games that do not show the real-life consequences of life and death instead generates more violence in males. Hunting helps develop a sense of self-mastery and impulse control in males that contributes to a healthy self-esteem. As Gurian says, "Hunting has proven to be across the spectrum—especially in those males we think of as violent, criminal males—as having great results in teaching those guys to hunt and getting them reoriented toward things they couldn't get in the inner city, so they even see a gun in a new way by learning to use it to hunt. It's why we are having success at places like Idaho Youth ranch. Places where boys are hardened criminals, but they'll kill an animal and hold it and weep."[1]

Dr. Randall Eaton is an award-winning author and behavioral scientist with an international reputation in wildlife conservation. During a recent conversation I had with Dr. Eaton, he told me,

> Hunting is one of the most transformative experiences a boy can have. Women are adapted to bring life into the world, but men are adapted to take life in order to support or protect life. I conducted thousands of surveys on older men and asked them to choose the life experience that most opened their hearts and engendered compassion in them. It was not becoming a parent, which was extremely high for women who had birthed a baby, nor was it teaching young people, nor the death of a loved one or beloved pet, but it was "taking the life of an animal."

According to Dr. Eaton, hunting makes men more compassionate and more peaceful. As he says, "Hunting and killing are as fundamental to male development as birthing and infant care are to women. . . . Men take life to support life, and the kill itself is the event that engenders compassion, respect for life, and the moral responsibility to protect it."[2] In his surveys of men who had hunted all their lives, the men overwhelmingly selected three universal virtues that they acquired from hunting: inner peace, patience, and humility. He cites Jimmy Carter and Nelson Mandela as just two of many famous men who are examples of both exemplary hunters and peacemakers.[3]

War is the only other activity that stimulates this kind of growth of compassion and empathy in males. Famous pioneer and frontiersman Davy Crockett learned a powerful lesson in compassion for human life during his experiences fighting in the Creek Indian Wars.[4]

Boys need to learn compassion for others or they become self-centered and self-focused. When that happens, other people in their lives suffer.

Consistency

Another aspect that contributes to a man's success is the ability to stay for the long haul. For instance, many professional baseball players become stars, but few make the Hall of Fame. Why? Because the difference between being good and being a Hall of Famer is *longevity*. It is being consistently good over a long period of time—not just good for a season or two. A baseball player who bats .300, with 30 home runs, and 100 runs batted in (RBIs) is a star. If he does that for ten years in a row he is a superstar, but that would probably not be good enough to get him into the Hall of Fame. However, if a player averaged those statistics for fifteen to twenty years, he would be guaranteed to make the Hall of Fame (provided he did not cheat).

Why is consistency important? It is important because our boys need to be men who stay consistent in their character over a lifetime. From experience I know it is easy to toe the line for a short period of time. But keeping my act together over the course of a lifetime has proven to be much more difficult. Boys who do not learn this discipline suffer by making self-defeating choices and decisions. Boys without consistency fall into situational ethics and other culturally acceptable traps. This sabotages not only their lives but those of their wives and children as well.

Whenever a politician makes a poor decision in his personal life, I hear people excuse his behavior by saying, "His personal life has no connection to his ability to do his job." Yes—it does! Character is character and it permeates a man's soul. It is not something that a man can apply in one area of his life and not in another, turning off and on like a light switch. If a man cheats, lies, and steals in his private life, it can be expected that he will do so in his professional life as well and vice versa.

Responsibility

> Failure to prepare is preparing to fail.
>
> John Wooden

Our culture has endured a profound change over the past several decades. Our children have become self-centered and self-focused. Former Notre Dame football coach Lou Holtz once said during a college football halftime television broadcast that the difference between young people when he coached and young people today is that they used to be concerned about their obligations and responsibilities. Now they are only concerned with their rights and privileges.

I hear too many young men today talk about their "rights." Young men in prison talk about their *rights* for television and recreation time not being met. High school students talk about their *rights* to wear the kind of clothing they want being denied. Terrorists try to destroy our country, then expect the same rights guaranteed under our Constitution.

246

Rights are intrinsic values guaranteed to people merely by virtue of being a human being. *Privileges* are things not guaranteed but that can be earned by hard work and responsibility. For instance, one of the reasons for our recent economic crash is that we made it a "right" instead of a privilege that everyone, regardless of whether they could afford it or had worked responsibly to earn it or not, be given the opportunity to own a house. That kind of philosophy is not what the economic underpinnings of our free market economy (the one that has been the *most* successful for the *most* amount of people throughout the history of the world) was built upon.

The truth is, there are not many "rights" in life. Most of the expectations young people are taught by the schools, media, and culture are in fact privileges and not rights. You do not have a right to own a big house, drive two new cars, and have a high-paying job with financial security. Children do have some rights—they have the right that any human being has to a loving, nurturing home, with adequate food, resources, and shelter from the elements. They probably even have a right for access to a decent education and basic health care. Beyond that, most other things are privileges—they are not guaranteed. Rights, at least in our country, are things guaranteed under the Constitution and Bill of Rights, such as the right to freedom and equality, free speech, or the right to bear arms. The last time I looked, the right to have a new car when you are sixteen, to have a television set in your room, to have a cell phone (or smart phone), to have a fancy gaming system in your room, and to have all the spending money you could ever want are not rights guaranteed under the Constitution. Those are privileges. We are fortunate enough to live in a country where we have the opportunity to *earn* privileges through hard work and dedication. In most other countries of the world, those opportunities are not available. However, children do not have a right to everything they want and desire, regardless of whether most of the other children in our culture have it or not.

Additionally, children (including teenagers) do not have the same privileges as adults do—they have not earned the right to have those privileges. Consequently, they do not have the right to go where they want, when they want, with whomever they want. If they live under your roof, they are still your responsibility. When they become self-sufficient adults living on their own, they will be entitled to whatever privileges they can afford and have worked responsibly to achieve. Therefore the only privileges they have in your home are those that you determine they have earned by exhibiting mature, responsible behavior. Too many parents are cowed into believing that if they take these privileges away from their children, they are somehow committing child abuse.

It's all part of the package of not sheltering our sons (or daughters) and of teaching them that anything they want in life is possible (at least in America—for now), provided they are willing to work hard for it. When we shelter young men from any kind of adversity and give them whatever their heart desires without making them work for it, we teach them unrealistic expectations from life. Then when they grow up and head out into the mean old world that does not care whether they have "rights" or not, they get disillusioned and angry because everything is not handed to them. Life is hard and boys who are not prepared to deal with it feel like failures. I've spoken to many parents of adult children who were raised in good homes but were failures and defeated by life. Upon reflection these parents admit they were too easy on their sons, giving them everything they needed and could possibly want. They did not teach them to be responsible.

Men with an attitude of entitlement make poor leaders of families and communities. They tend to be selfish and self-focused.

Hardihood

Hardihood is a word you don't hear much anymore. But it is a quality I not only admire in other men but continually strive for in my own life. It means having fortitude (another word you don't hear much today), courage, and internal strength. Dictionary.com gives the definition of *hardihood* as: (1) boldness or courage, daring; (2) audacity or imprudence; (3) strength, power, vigor; and (4) hardy spirit or character, fortitude. Young men who exhibit the character trait of hardihood have a boldness and confidence in their actions, especially when encountering difficulties or dangers. They have a stout and persistent courage, mental toughness, and physical endurance. They resist fatigue and are somewhat daring in nature.

I have a friend who has been going through some of the most difficult struggles I can imagine for years now. I do not know how he keeps going, but he is still standing tall, leading his family despite facing overwhelming odds that would have crushed most men. He has more hardiness and fortitude than any man I have ever met. I cannot tell you how much I admire him.

This quality prevents men from being passive and indecisive, two traits that are weakening males throughout our culture, making them ineffective leaders and less than they are capable of becoming. Life *will* be hard, and I want a man in my daughter's life who does not quit the first (or tenth) time he encounters the storms of life.

Passion

I admire men, particularly young men, who are passionate about something—especially if they are passionate about a worthy cause. Passion is a rare quality in a man. Oh, I know men who are passionate about golfing, hunting or fishing, or NASCAR, but to be passionate about things that matter in life is a rare trait in men.

My friend is passionate about his sport. He trains daily and competes regularly. He spends significant amounts of time and money on his hobby or passion. He's a good guy, but when asked to volunteer with our fatherless boy program, he doesn't have the time. When asked for a donation for our Single Mom's Family Camps, he says he doesn't have any spare money. Frankly, he doesn't seem very passionate about his wife or children either.

If we judge the things we are passionate about by the amount of time we spend on them, what would others say we are passionate about? And even more than that, is our passion invested in a good and worthy cause?

Healthy passion keeps men from being complacent and passive, two of the great emasculators of manhood.

Chivalry

Chivalry seems to be dead today, or as my editor put it, "has been stomped to death." She grew up in Texas and thinks a good old Texas cowboy may be one of the last bastions of chivalry left. Maybe so, but most of the cowboys I've met at rodeos seem to be real "hound dogs," if you know what I mean (no offense, guys). Nevertheless, she has a valid point—you don't see many examples of chivalry today. Frankly, most young men today are not forced to earn the affections of young women—much to the girls' detriment. But if you want your son to marry well and be successful in life, teaching him the art of chivalry will be to his advantage.

By my example with my wife, I taught my daughter that she should expect a man to open all doors for her, especially her car door. My son just naturally assumes that his role as a man requires him to treat women and children a certain way—with respect and gallantry. Many dates I watched out the living room window as my daughter stood outside the passenger side car door while the young man got in the car, started it, realized his error, and ran around the car to open her door for her. She used that yardstick as one way to judge the quality of a young man who was interested in her. I believe that it is important for a girl to be in a choosing mode when selecting a young man, not a settling mode. Therefore it requires that a young man *earn* her heart through his actions. Chivalry is one way he earns her admiration and shows her he cares about and respects her. I stated earlier in this book that it is important to judge a man by his actions and not his words. Since we know that all of us are on our best behavior while we are dating, a man who has lax manners and lack of respect during the dating process can be guaranteed to slip even lower after the vows are said.

Chivalry is more than just manners; it is a way of life. The way a person dresses and conducts himself day to day speaks volumes about his character. Is cleanliness next to godliness? I don't know, but I do know I don't

251

want a stinky guy for a son-in-law and the father of my grandchildren. I also want to observe how a young man interested in my daughter treats those around him. How does he treat me and my wife? Is he respectful without being obsequious? How does he treat his own parents? How does he treat animals and people who are socially undervalued (a waitress, a mentally retarded child, an elderly person, a street panhandler)?

How about his speech? Is he contemptuous of others? Is he negative? Does he take joy in others' failings? Does he think he's better than others (or worse than others)? Does he go out of his way to run over a squirrel in the road? Does he have an entitlement mentality? What kind of music does he listen to and what TV shows does he watch? His attitude in those areas will in part determine whether his actions are chivalrous or cowardly.

I want a young man for my daughter who treats her with respect and dignity. Who cherishes and honors her—a man who will protect her while at the same time encourage and nourish her to be all that she is capable of. I want a man who will bring out the best woman, wife, and mother my daughter can be. I want a man who is capable of finishing the job I started.

Intelligence

Intelligence consists of a number of factors, including sound judgment, practical common sense, intuition, adaptability, rational thought, and analytic and cognitive abilities. Likely, the desire to continue to learn and improve oneself is an important factor in being intelligent.

In 1983, psychologist Howard Gardner developed his theory of multiple intelligences, which maintains there exist many different types of "intelligences" ascribed to human beings. His original list consisted of seven categories, with an eighth added later:

1. Kinesthetic—has to do with body movement and physiology; e.g., athletes, dancers
2. Interpersonal—are extroverts who work well in groups; e.g., salespeople, politicians, teachers
3. Verbal-Linguistic—proficient with words and languages; e.g., writers, public speakers, philosophers
4. Intrapersonal—good at understanding self; e.g., psychologists, theologians
5. Logical-Mathematical—abstract reasoning and numbers; e.g., scientists, doctors, economists
6. Visual-Spatial—hand-eye coordination and puzzle solving; e.g., artists, engineers, architects
7. Musical—adept at music and rhythm; e.g., musicians, singers, composers
8. Naturalist—sensitive to nature; e.g., farmers, gardeners, naturalists, conservationists

Since then a number of other intelligences have been suggested but excluded including spiritual, existential, and moral intelligences.[5]

One of the advantages of understanding differing intelligences, rather than just relying on someone's book learning or fact retention, is that people can be gifted in one area and not in another. It does not mean they are not intelligent. For instance, someone like Albert Einstein who is brilliant in logical-mathematical intelligence may not be able to speak well or relate to others successfully. We know from his example that he is anything but unintelligent.

One of the great disservices we do with males is not encouraging them to keep learning throughout their lives.

Many men finish school and never pick up another book their entire lives. Most men don't attend seminars or workshops that grow them or teach them new things—especially if they involve relationship skills.

That's just my partial list of qualities I want in the young man who will marry my daughter. There are probably a lot of intangibles I left out. For instance, it is difficult to judge the "heart" of a young man. And his heart may be the most important attribute he possesses. One thing I have observed is that the quality of the young man seems to be in direct proportion to the character of his parents and the upbringing he was given. Not always, but most of the time. Sometimes children make poor choices and go off the deep end despite being raised under the best of circumstances. But most frequently, the apple doesn't fall far from the tree. If you want to raise a young man of character, compassion, and depth, then you and his father need to be people who exhibit those qualities in every area of your life.

And so concludes our quest to discover how to finish the final push of a boy in the journey toward manhood. I hope that you have recognized the joys to be found in parenting a teenage boy. While challenging, this is a wonderful time of life that gives us as adults many opportunities to instill important life lessons that will allow us to "finish strong" in our role as parents. At least that's what we think—but wait! Just when the last teenager grows up and moves away . . . here come grandchildren! And the adventure begins anew!

Truthfully we never stop being parents. Our roles just change when our children become adults. There's a saying,

"Grandchildren are God's gifts to parents for not killing their children." I certainly hope so. Have fun!

Questions for Reflection and Discussion

1. Why is it important to teach young men to respect females?

2. Why do boys need to learn the value of hard work—or do they?

3. What are some ways to teach your son the gift of having compassion for others?

4. Chivalry is often thought of as old-fashioned and out of date in our culture. Why or why not is the concept of chivalry important to young males?

NOTES

Introduction

1. Patrick Morley, *The Young Man in the Mirror* (Nashville: Broadman & Holman, 2003), 76–77.

Chapter 1 His Changing Body and Mind

1. Michael Gurian, *A Fine Young Man* (New York: Tarcher/Putnam, 1999), 77.

2. Robert May, *The Case for Sex Differences: Sex and Fantasy—Patterns of Male and Female Development* (New York: Norton, 1980).

3. "Boys and Puberty," 4Parents.Gov, http://www.4parents.gov/sexdevt/boysmen/boyspuberty/index.html, revised March 27, 2009.

4. "Boys Growing Up," BBC Science & Nature, January 8, 2010, http://www.bbc.co.uk/science/humanbody/body/articles/lifecycle/teenagers/boy_s_growth.shtml.

5. Michael Gurian, *The Wonder of Boys* (New York: Jeremy P. Tarcher/Putnam, 1996), 11.

6. Joshua S. Goldstein, *War and Gender: How Gender Shapes the War System and Vice Versa* (Cambridge, UK: Cambridge University Press, 2001), chapter 3, attributed to Mazur and Booth 1998; Mazur and Lamb 1980; Booth et al. 1989; Archer 1991, 17–18; Geen 1998, 321; Blum 1997, 167; Turner 1994, 246; Baron and Richardson 1994, 257; Klama 1988, 77; fans: Bernhardt et al. 1998; lawyers: Dabbs, in *Science*, April 26, 1991: 513. http://www.warandgender.com/wgmaleag.htm#FN03_49.

7. Gurian, *Fine Young Man*, 38–39.

8. Ibid., 38–40.

9. Gurian, *Wonder of Boys*, 19.

10. Gurian, *Fine Young Man*, chap. 2.

11. Edmund Morris, *The Rise of Theodore Roosevelt* (New York: The Modern Library, 1979).

Chapter 2 Communicating with Teen Boys

1. Albert Mehrabian and Susan R. Ferris, "Inference of Attitudes from Nonverbal Communication in Two Channels," *Journal of Consulting Psychology* 31, no. 3 (June 1967): 248–58.

2. Gurian, *Wonder of Boys*, 16.

3. "Pupils Must Look Away to Think," BBC News, January 11, 2006, http://news.bbc.co.uk/2/hi/uk_news/education/4602178.stm.

4. John T. Molloy, *Why Men Marry Some Women and Not Others* (New York: Warner, 2003), 124.

Chaper 3 Mom and Son

1. Paul Coughlin, *Unleashing Courageous Faith* (Grand Rapids: Bethany, 2009), 20.

2. Ibid., 55.

3. Aubrey Andelin, *Man of Steel and Velvet* (Pierce City, MO: Pacific Press Santa Barbara, 1972), 31, original emphasis.

4. Rick Johnson, *The Power of a Man* (Grand Rapids: Revell, 2009), 191–92.

5. Robert E. Howard, ". . . and their memory was a bitter tree . . .": *Queen of the Black Coast & Others*, ed. Tim Underwood (Nevada City, CA: Blackbart Books, 2008), 407.

Chapter 4 Dad and Son

1. Rick Johnson, "Is There a Difference in Educational Outcomes in Students from Single Parent Homes?" A Thesis Presented to the Graduate Program in Partial Fulfillment of the Requirements for the Degree of Masters in Education, Concordia University, Portland, OR, November 2009.

2. Most of this section adapted from *The Power of a Man*, chap. 5.

3. Rogers Wright and Nicholas Cummings, eds., *Destructive Trends in Mental Health: The Well-Intentioned Path to Harm* (New York: Routledge, 2005).

4. Morris, *Rise of Theodore Roosevelt*, 11–12.

5. Ibid., 32.

6. Ibid., 13.

Chapter 5 Healthy Masculinity

1. Gurian, *Wonder of Boys*, 29.

2. Andelin, *Man of Steel and Velvet*, 9.

3. Ibid.

4. Ibid., 13.

5. "Bob Marley," Wikipedia, December 30, 2009, http://en.wikipedia.org/wiki/Bob_Marley.

Chapter 7 Dangers

1. Gurian, *Fine Young Man*, 277.

2. William Pollock, PhD, *Real Boys: Rescuing Our Sons from the Myths of Boyhood* (New York: Henry Holt & Co., 1998), xxi.

3. Gurian, *Wonder of Boys*, 183.

4. "Understanding and Raising Boys: Boys in School," PBS Parents, http://www.pbs.org/parents/raisingboys/school.html.

5. "More Statistics about Boys and Boyhood: Boys and School," Supporting Our Sons. Note on sources: The majority of these statistics have been culled from two books: Dr. William Pollock, *Real Boys*, and Drs. Dan Kindlon and Michael Thompson, *Raising Cain: Protecting the Emotional Life of Boys*. For further information on the statistics above, feel free to contact us at members@supportingoursons.org; http://www.supportingoursons.org/misc/moreinfo.cfm.

6. Peg Tyre, "Report Card on Boys Troubling," *Chicago Tribune*, October 13, 2008. Read more at Suite101.com: "A Nation of Boys At-Risk: Statistics on Boys and School Are Very Disturbing"; http://educationalissues.suite101.com/article.cfm/a_nation_of_boys_atrisk#ixzz0d2etjIkN.

7. James Dobson, *Bringing Up Boys* (Wheaton: Tyndale, 2001), 33–34.

8. Gleaned from Paul Coughlin, "Bullying Defined," Crosswalk.com, http://www.crosswalk.com/parenting/11595601/.

9. Ibid.

10. John Eldredge, *Wild at Heart* (Nashville: Thomas Nelson, 2001), 80.

11. Christina Hoff Sommers, *The War against Boys* (New York: Simon & Schuster, 2000), 1.

12. Randall Eaton, *From Boys to Men of Heart: Hunting as a Rite of Passage* (Shelton, WA: OWLink Media, 2009), 59.

13. See American Youth Policy Forum, *Whatever It Takes: How Twelve Communities Are Reconnecting Out-of-School Youth*, page 1, "Every Nine Seconds in America a Student Becomes a Dropout," http://www.aypf.org/publications/WhateverItTakes/WIT_nineseconds.pdf.

Research presented by J. P. Greene and M. A. Winters during a Connect for Kids and National Education Association conference call on the Dropout Crisis (February 2005) found the African American graduation rate in 2002 to be 56%, Latinos 52%, and Whites 78%.

14. Katharin Peter, Laura Horn, C. Dennis Carroll, "Gender Differences in Participation and Completion of Undergraduate Education and How They Have Changed Over Time," Postsecondary Education Descriptive Analysis Reports, National Center for Education Statistics, US Department of Education, February 2005, 7.

15. "Projections of Education Statistics to 2013," National Center for Education Statistics, US Department of Education, October 2003, figure 14.

16. Gurian, *Fine Young Man*, 14–15, 17.

17. "Understanding and Raising Boys: Boys in School," PBS Parents, http://www.pbs.org/parents/raisingboys/school.html.

18. "More Schools Test Single-Sex Classrooms," MSNBC US News & Education, July 6, 2006, http://www.msnbc.msn.com/id/13229488/.

19. Urvia McDowell, MS, and Ted G. Futris, PhD, "Adolescents at Risk: Illicit Drug Use," FLM-FS-15-02, Family Life Month Packet 2002, Family and Consumer Sciences, Campbell Hall, CFLE, Department of Human Development and Family Science, Ohio State University, http://ohioline.osu.edu/flm02/FS15.html.

20. Ibid.

21. Adolescent Substance Abuse Knowledge Base, various studies performed by the National Household Survey on Drug Abuse (NHSDA), http://www.adolescent-substance-abuse.com/state-stats.html.

22. Methamphetamine, http://en.wikipedia.org/wiki/Methamphetamine.

23. Substance Abuse and Mental Health Services Administration, *The Relationship between Family Structure and Adolescent Substance Use* (Rockville, MD: National Clearinghouse for Alcohol and Drug Information, 1996).

24. R. E. Denton and C. M. Kampfe, "The Relationship between Family Variables and Adolescent Substance Abuse: A Literature Review," *Adolescence* 114 (1994): 475–95.

25. US Department of Health and Human Services, *Survey on Child Health* (Washington, DC: National Center for Health Statistics; GPO,1993).

26. J. Hoffman and R. Johnson, "A National Portrait of Family Structure and Adolescent Drug Use," *Journal of Marriage and the Family* 60 (1998): 633–45.

27. R. Wedgeworth, "State of Adult Literacy in 2004, ProLiteracy President's State of Literact Report 2004," http://www.proliteracy.org/NetCommunity/Document.Doc?id=12.

28. Demographics, http://medicine.creighton.edu/idc242/2005/Group6/Demographics.htm.

29. US Department of Justice, Office of Justice Programs, Bureau of Justice Statistics, spreadsheet "National Data—Number of Arrests for Violent Crimes (juveniles under 18)," and spreadsheet "Arrests by Age Group, 1970–1999," http://www.ojp.usdoj.gov/bjs/dtdata.htm.

30. C. Harper and S. Lanahan, "Father Absence and Youth Incarceration," Working Paper #99-03, Center for Research on Child Well-Being, Princeton University, 1999.

31. Phil Chalmers, *Inside the Mind of a Teen Killer* (Nashville: Thomas Nelson, 2009), 17.

32. Ibid., 23.

33. Ibid., 16–17, 62.

Chapter 8 Developing a Healthy Sexuality

1. J. C. Abma et al., "Teenagers in the United States: Sexual Activity, Contraceptive Use, and Childbearing, 2002," *Vital and Health Statistics*, 2004, series 23, no. 24, http://www.guttmacher.org/pubs/fb_ATSRH.html.

2. Ibid.

3. National Campaign to Prevent Teen Pregnancy. (2004). Factsheet: How is the 34% statistic calculated? Washington, DC: Author.

4. R. A. Maynard, ed., *Kids Having Kids: A Robin Hood Foundation Special Report on the Costs of Adolescent Childbearing* (New York: Robin Hood Foundation, 1996).

5. The Annie E. Casey Foundation, *2004 Kids Count Data Book: Moving Youth from Risk to Opportunity*, Baltimore, MD, P11.

6. Centers for Disease Control (CDC), "Unmarried Childbearing, Final Data for 2005, Tables C and 18," National Center for Health Statistics, 2009, http://www.cdc.gov/nchs/FASTATS/unmarry.htm.

7. Johnson, "Is There a Difference in Educational Outcomes?"

8. Child Trends, *Facts at a Glance,* Publication #2006-03, Kaiser Family Foundation, 2006, http://www.kff.org/womenshealth/upload/3040-03.pdf.

9. Centers for Disease Control and Prevention, "Genital HPV Infection. Online Fact Sheet." Retrieved May 9, 2005 from http://www.cdc.gov/std/HPV/STDFact-HPV.htm.

10. CDC, "Sexually Transmitted Disease Surveillance," Kaiser Family Foundation, 2004, http://www.kff.org/womenshealth/upload/3040-03.pdf.

11. H. Weinstock, S. Berman, and W. Cates Jr., "Sexually Transmitted Diseases among American Youth: Incidence and Prevalence Estimates, 2000," *Perspectives on Sexual and Reproductive Health* 36 (2004): 6–10.

12. J. R. Cates, N. L. Herndon, S. L. Schulz, and J. E. Darroch, *Our Voices, Our Lives, Our Futures: Youth and Sexually Transmitted Diseases* (Chapel Hill, NC: University of North Carolina at Chapel Hill School of Journalism and Mass Communication, 2004).

13. Jeff Purkiss, *Squires to Knights: Mentoring Our Teenage Boys* (N.p.: Xulon Press, 2007), 44–45.

14. Bill Taverner and Sue Montfort, "Making Sense of Abstinence: Lessons for Comprehensive Sex Education," The Center for Family Education, Planned Parenthood of Greater Northern New Jersey, 2005, 61.

15. Jerry Ropelato, Internet Pornography Statistics, http://www.internet-filter-review.toptenreviews.com/internet-pornography-statistics.html, retrieved January 2006.

16. AWARE, "Illusions: Uncovering the Truth about Pornography," Facilitators Guide, 2007,18.

17. AWARE, Help 4 Parents, "Attracted or Addicted: Are Your Kids on a Ride They Can't Get Off?" *Cheap Thrills*, 7.

18. Adapted from Mark B. Kastleman, *The Drug of the New Millennium: The Science of How Internet Pornography Radically Alters the Human Brain and Body* (Orem, UT: Granite Publishing Co., 2001).

19. Stephen Arterburn and Fred Stoecker with Mike Yorkey, *Every Man's Battle* (Colorado Springs: WaterBrook, 2000), 63.

Chapter 9 Spiritual Legacy

1. Eaton, *From Boys to Men of Heart*, 59.

2. David Kinnaman and Gabe Lyons, *unChristian* (Grand Rapids: Baker, 2007), 26.

3. David Murrow, *Why Men Hate Going to Church* (Nashville: Thomas Nelson, 2005), 6.

4. Ibid.

5. Paul Coughlin, *No More Christian Nice Guy* (Grand Rapids: Bethany, 2005), 34.

6. Coughlin, *Unleashing Courageous Faith*, 142.

7. Ibid.

8. Some Guy, Albert Einstein quotes, 2006, http://www.some-guy.com/quotes/einstein.html#relativity.

Chapter 10 Building Character for a Lifetime

1. Andelin, *Man of Steel and Velvet*, 169.

2. William Shakespeare, *Hamlet*, Act II, scene ii.

3. "50 Cent: Father Figure?" The Best of Men, http://www.thebestofmen.com/fatherhood.htm, accessed June 13, 2006.

4. Martin Luther King Jr., "The Purpose of Education" Speech, Morehouse College, 1948.

Chapter 11 Self-Discipline

1. Andelin, *Man of Steel and Velvet*, 169.

2. Ibid., 171–72.

3. Credit Card Debt Statistics, Money-Zine.com, http://www.money-zine.com/Financial-Planning/Debt-Consolidation/Credit-Card-Debt-Statistics/.

4. Financial Literacy Statistics, Young Americans Center for Financial Education, http://www.yacenter.org/index.cfm?fuseAction=financialLiteracyStatistics.financialLiteracyStatistics.

5. "27 Money Tips for College Students, Get Rich Slowly," August 30, 2006, http://www.getrichslowly.org/blog/2006/08/30/27-money-tips-for-college-students/.

6. "College Student Credit Card," http://www.collegestudentcreditcard.com/articles6.html.

Chapter 12 Leadership

1. Coughlin, *Unleashing Courageous Faith*, 19.

2. Email from Tony Rorie, June 2009, used by permission.

3. Purkiss, *Squires to Knights*, chap. 1.

4. John Eldredge, *The Way of the Wild Heart: A Map for the Masculine Journey* (Nashville: Thomas Nelson, 2006), 6.

5. Robert Lewis, *Raising a Modern-Day Knight: A Father's Role in Guiding His Son to Authentic Manhood* (Wheaton: Tyndale, 1997), 99.

6. Ibid., 51–59.

7. Coughlin, *No More Christian Nice Guy*, 126.

8. Andelin, *Man of Steel and Velvet*, 12.

9. Gurian, *Wonder of Boys*, 30.

10. Andelin, *Man of Steel and Velvet*, 155.

11. See "NIDA InfoFacts: Steroids (Anabolic-Androgenic)," National Institute on Drug Abuse, http://www.drugabuse.gov/infofacts/steroids.html.

12. "Are Steroids Worth the Risk?" Teens Health, December 22, 2009, http://www.kidshealth.org/teen/exercise/safety/steroids.html.

Chapter 13 Things Your Son Needs to Know to Court My Daughter

1. "Respect and Responsibility: The Truth about Kids Who Hunt," DVD recording, produced by Randall Eaton, PhD, 1997.

2. Eaton, *From Boys to Men of Heart*, xlix.

3. Ibid.

4. Documentary, "Hunter Heroes: Daniel Boone and Davy Crockett," The History Channel, September 28, 2009.

5. "Intelligence," Wikipedia, http://en.wikipedia.org/wiki/Intelligence.

Bestselling author and speaker **Rick Johnson** founded Better Dads, a fathering skills program based on the urgent need to empower men to lead and serve in their families and communities. Rick's books have expanded his ministry to include influencing the whole family, with life-changing insights for men and women on parenting, marriage, and personal growth. He is a sought-after speaker at many large conferences across the United States and Canada and is a popular keynote speaker at men's and women's retreats and conferences on parenting and marriage. Rick is also a nationally recognized expert in several areas, including the effects of fatherlessness, and has been asked to teach at various educational venues.

To find out more about Rick Johnson, his books, and the Better Dads ministry, or to schedule workshops, seminars, or speaking engagements, please visit www.betterdads .net.

Meet

RICK JOHNSON

at www.BetterDads.net

Connect with Rick on Facebook

 *Rick Johnson*

DON'T MISS THESE OTHER GREAT TITLES

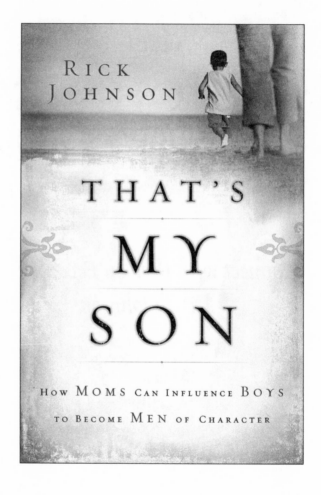

RICK JOHNSON

THAT'S MY SON

HOW MOMS CAN INFLUENCE BOYS TO BECOME MEN OF CHARACTER

A mother's imprint on her son lasts forever.

Revell
a division of Baker Publishing Group
www.RevellBooks.com

FROM FAMILY EXPERT
RICK JOHNSON!

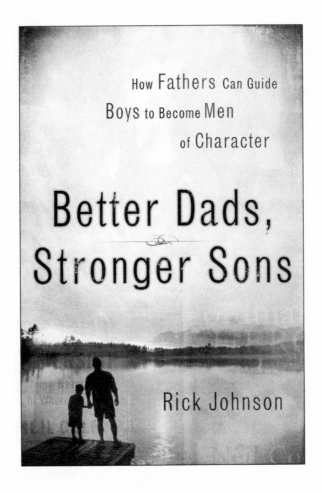

How Fathers Can Guide
Boys to Become Men
of Character

Better Dads,
Stronger Sons

Rick Johnson

Encourages and empowers fathers in their important role.

YOUR RECIPE FOR MARITAL SUCCESS

Learn how to use your differences to add spice and
passion to your marriage.

INSPIRE YOUR MAN TO GREATNESS

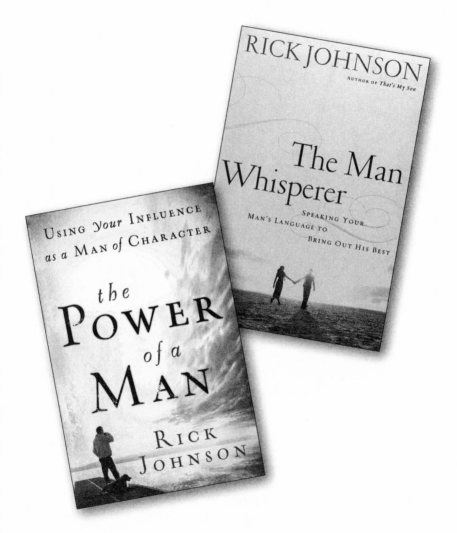